S 5/13

URE

**ng Guide to
n People**

DIRECTORY OF SOCIAL CHANGE

Published by
Directory of Social Change
24 Stephenson Way
London NW1 2DP
Tel. 08450 77 77 07; Fax 020 7391 4804
E-mail publications@dsc.org.uk
www.dsc.org.uk
from whom further copies and a full books catalogue are available.

Directory of Social Change is a Registered Charity no. 800517

First published 2007

ISBN: 978 1 903991 85 5

British Library Cataloguing in Publication Data
A catalogue record for this book is available from the British Library

Illustrations by Grizelda
Cover designed by Kate Bass and Simon Parkin
Typeset by Linda Parker
Printed and bound by Page Bros., Norwich

All other Directory of Social Change departments in London:
08450 77 77 07

Directory of Social Change Northern Office:
Federation House, Hope Street, Liverpool L1 9BW
Courses and conferences 08450 77 77 07
Research 0151 708 0136

Contents

Dedication

To my staff at DSC who are mostly a pleasure!!!

Acknowledgements

Thank you to the following who teach me every day how much people are willing and able to give when they care: our DSC team as at March 2007.

Reda Allam

John Barrett

Kate Bass

Fred Carpenter

Claire Cohen

Charles Collett

Kirsty Cunningham

Justine Fernandes

Sandra Fielding

Alan French

Conor Gibson

Kim Hobbs

Supriya Horn

Annette Hutchinson

Jay Kennedy

Kajol Kochar

Richard Lee

Graham Leigh

Denise Lillya

John Martin

Michael McManus

Sarah Johnston

Lucy Muir-Smith

Shireen Mustafa

Sujata Pearson

Maria Pemberton

Harin Perera

Satinder Pujji

Helen Rice

Amy Rosser

Carole Sandman

Cathy Shimmin

Ruby Smallin

John Smyth

Rachel Stephens

Jill Thornton

Tom Traynor

Lisa van der Wekken

John Wallace

Ben Wittenberg

About the author

Debra Allcock Tyler is Chief Executive of the Directory of Social Change (DSC), which campaigns for an independent voluntary sector at the heart of social change. DSC achieves this through publishing, training and commentary. Current campaigns include the need to promote transparency and accountability of the sector, the need to increase public confidence in charitable organisations and concern about the sector's independence from government. With an annual turnover of more than £3 million, DSC has contact with some 20,000 voluntary and community organisations every year through its programmes.

Debra works with boards, chief executives and their top teams in governance issues, leadership, vision, mission, values and the establishment of strategic objectives. She is a trustee of MedicAlert® which is the only non-profit-making, registered charity providing a life-saving identification system for individuals with hidden medical conditions and allergies.

She is a member of the SORP Committee, a Fellow of the Royal Society for the encouragement of Arts, Manufactures & Commerce (FRSA) and a Licensed Practitioner of NLP. She is a Special Ambassador for the Guides Association (now Girlguiding UK) and a member of the Advisory Panel for the MSc in Voluntary Sector Management at Cass Business School, City University. She was a member of the Buse Commission for self-regulation in fundraising. She has a BSc (Hons) in Psychology, a Certificate in Natural Sciences (Physics; Chemistry; Earth Sciences; Biological Sciences) and is currently studying for a BSc in Physics.

During her twenty-two year career, Debra has worked in insurance, management consultancy and the voluntary sector, carrying out a range of managerial and leadership roles including sales, product development, campaigning, media relations and training.

She is an internationally published author of several books covering topics such as leadership, management, communication skills, personal development and time management, and has made many appearances on radio, TV and in the press.

Introduction

This is a book about people. That sounds like a big topic and indeed it is. Specifically, it's about people in the workplace: how they behave, their impact on you, and your impact on them. This book is not aimed specifically at managers. It is very much for anyone who has to work with people (most of us I imagine) at any level in an organisation. But if you are a manager reading this book, I hope that you find the general observations and ideas useful in helping you to think about how you lead and manage teams.

I base my observations and thoughts in this book on a number of different sources: stories that people have told me; my own work experience at all levels in an organisation; my research and training; and my psychology degree, which I took as a mature student, not so much because I wanted to understand more about others, but because I wanted to have a better insight into myself – and inevitably I found out not just about myself, but also about what makes other people tick.

During my 20-plus years in the workplace I have realised a basic truth about most human beings: they are largely influenced not by facts, not by evidence, not by logic, but by their emotions. And yet there are still so many people in the world who believe that all you need to do win others over to your argument is to present a strong, clear and evidence-based case. But if that is true, how is it that smokers still smoke, drivers still speed and directors of fundraising refuse point blank to get their expense forms in on time? Because logic doesn't drive us. It can inform our thinking, it can help to clarify what we want to do, but ultimately it is not what determines our decision making.

It is because we forget this basic fact about human beings that we so often get it wrong in how we communicate with them. I remember a colleague I used to work with saying to me that she could not argue with the logic of the position I had presented to her and she didn't have a better suggestion – but that what I had said just didn't *feel* right. And because her emotions weren't engaged by my persuasive arguments, her incentive to make it work was diminished. So the initiative I had proposed and asked her to deliver didn't work terribly well. There's no point saying, 'Well, she should have done it anyhow!' The truth is that if people's hearts aren't engaged then their heads are not going to compensate.

For example, I am currently studying for a degree in physics. When people hear that, they automatically assume that a) I must be really clever and b) I must be driven by evidence, experiment, empirical data and logical, proven arguments.

Well, first off, being interested in a subject doesn't necessarily make you good at it – I love it but I don't find it easy! And, second, it is not the facts themselves that drive this strange passion of mine, it is how the facts and figures that inevitably come with science make me *feel*. I feel alternately excited, challenged and frustrated when I'm getting to grips with a relatively simple maths problem or when I'm struggling to factorise. It's not the cold, hard facts that inspire me, but the way they make me think and feel. Lifeless facts don't move people. The emotions those facts stir up do.

So this book attempts to give you information, facts, theories and stories that hopefully will help you to understand a little more about yourself, and, perhaps more importantly in the context of working with people, also about others and how their feelings can create an effective working environment.

I don't pretend to have all the answers or even that my suggestions are the right ones for you. Any advice I give or observations I make are very much my own conclusions based on my opinion of what I have studied or observed – you are free to disregard those that simply don't fit in with your own experience. The book simply takes a number of different approaches to working with other people which you may or may not find useful.

There is a multitude of books on the subject of what makes human beings tick, from seminal psychological texts such as Eric Berne's *Games People Play* to the more 'pop psychology' ones like *How to Make Friends and Influence People* or *Emotional Intelligence*. I list those I find most useful or credible in the bibliography at the back of this book.

But I would strongly recommend three books in particular to you. The first is Stephen Pinker's *How the Mind Works*, which is the most useful summary of how human beings think, feel and react that I have ever read. The second is Dylan Evans's book *Emotion: the Science of Sentiment*. The third is the wonderful text by Theodore Zeldin called *Conversation: How Talk Can Change Your Life*.

Oh, and if work and the people in it are really driving you to despair, then read Scott Adams's *The Dilbert Principle*, which is bone-shakingly funny and helps to put all of our workplace woes into perspective.

Finally, I am not trying to convince you that it's straightforward or that the ideas and tools work all the time with all people – frankly, sometimes they don't. So my advice with this book is just to try out some of the ideas and see if they work. If they don't, then try something else.

People are generally not all that bad – honest! And if you make the effort to see things from their point of view you'll be amazed and delighted at how you can turn the pain of working with them into a real pleasure.

1 What makes people human

Seek first to understand, before being understood.

St Francis of Assisi

Outcomes

After reading this chapter you will:
- **Understand how and why people are different**
- **Know how to deal with assumptions**
- **Understand why people appear to be deluding themselves**

We can't really know how to work effectively with others without understanding human nature. And we can't examine the nature of human beings without taking a little excursion into the whole 'nature/nurture' debate. Is human nature innate or nurtured? This question still keeps rearing its ugly head, even though I have to say that for me it's fairly straightforward. It's both of course. Human beings may be born with a predisposition to a certain type of behaviour but it's the environment that will allow that behaviour to materialise – it's not inevitable that it will.

To put this into some context I want to talk a little about whether our genetic make-up is a fundamental determinant of what we are like when we grow up.

There is a genetic condition called phenylketonurea (PKU).[1] This condition means that you have a spontaneously occurring mutation in a gene which results in a defective protein. The particular protein is unable to convert phenylalanine to tyrosine and so too much phenylalanine remains in the blood. If PKU is untreated it can result in reduced brain development and irreversible mental retardation. However, the condition only develops if the environment supports it – that is if phenylalanine is present in the diet. If a child is diagnosed with PKU early enough in life and phenylalanine is eliminated from their diet (e.g. by avoiding eating meat) then the symptoms do not manifest themselves. Indeed, successful treatments for PKU mean that adults with the condition do not need to continue avoiding phenylalanine in their diets. So this is a classic case of a genetic condition which is dependent upon the environment in order to manifest itself.

However, it is really important for you to know that genes in themselves do not actually produce specific behaviours. All genes do is code for proteins and it is the action of the proteins that causes biological and behavioural traits. Most

---

[1] T. Whatson and V. Stirling (eds) (1998), *Development and Flexibility (Biology: Brain & Behaviour, 2)*, Springer-Verlag/Open University Press, pp. 122–123.

genes represent only a small beginning in a bigger story of interacting hormones, proteins, chemicals and so on, which are influenced by diet, environment and society.

Even those things that we take as a basic biological given are not necessarily free from environmental influences, for example, the ability to see. Experiments on mice and cats have shown that if you blindfold an otherwise perfectly healthy mouse or cat from birth so that it can't see, it completely loses the ability to see even though there is nothing actually physically wrong. This is because the eye needs to learn how to see.[2]

It is true, therefore, that your environment and your physical self do have an enormous effect on your behaviour. However, unlike the poor cats and mice in the example above, we do have some control over our environment and we have the ability to take control of our behavioural responses to situations in which we find ourselves. Technically, when we say to ourselves, 'I can't help it, it's just the way I am', we are telling ourselves a bit of a fib. The reality is that in most cases we really can help it and our behaviour can become a choice. And that is an amazingly liberating thought, I think. You do not have to be trapped by your psychology. You can choose the behaviours and thinking which are going to work best for you to a much greater extent than you might imagine.

I saw this principle in action when I spent some time working with an organisation called Youth at Risk (YAR). YAR works with young people who have been socially excluded. They often have had very troubled childhoods, and have learned not to trust adults – or even themselves really. Many have been physically, emotionally or mentally abused in some way and a high proportion end up on the 'other side' of what most of us would consider to be social norms.

YAR helps these young people by showing them that their past does not have to dictate their present or their future. Being a victim in the past does not mean you have to be a victim in the future. You can make choices about who you want to be and what you want to do, and you don't need to blame those choices on others. You can't undo what has happened in the past, but you can change what you do for the future. The young people find this way of thinking liberates their ability to make choices about their lives, but it can be hard work.

The starting point is being self-aware: understanding that your past can influence your decisions today and dictate your future unless you consciously decide not to let this happen. Unfortunately, for many of us we are simply reacting to situations that we find ourselves in without necessarily fully understanding why.

Different or the same?

It is one of the strange paradoxes of human existence that we have to recognise that other people are the same as us and yet profoundly different. So what does that mean exactly? Well, for me it means beginning by recognising that there are some things that almost every human being on the planet has in common.

---

[2] T. Whatson and V. Stirling (eds) (1998), *Development and Flexibility (Biology: Brain & Behaviour, 2)*, Springer-Verlag/Open University Press, pp. 94–99.

We all:

- Want to be loved
- Want to be able to love
- Want to feel that we 'belong'
- Want our efforts to be appreciated
- Want to be liked
- Want to feel that we are in control of our lives
- Want to feel that we have choices
- Want to feel that we are decent people
- Want to be good at something
- Want to be recognised for being good at it
- Want our voice to be heard
- Want to be understood

So fundamentally our needs are much the same. However, what makes us different is the way in which those needs are met. For example, some people want to be the best at what they do: they have a drive to be expert or the most knowledgeable about something. Others just want to feel that they have done their best and they don't feel the need to outshine others. As an aside, interestingly, I've noticed that for those people whom we term 'ambitious' at work, we tend to view that term, and therefore that person, negatively. Yet we consider ambition in a professional footballer or racing driver, for example, as a good thing. This may be because we find it an attractive quality in competitive sport because most of us don't have that talent or aim, but in the workplace we feel equality matters more.

But back to the point in hand. If we are faced with a situation that doesn't allow us to meet our common needs, as listed above, it will most likely cause a negative reaction to whatever we are observing or hearing. If we feel that our efforts at work haven't been appreciated by our boss we are likely to perceive that individual with some negativity. If we feel that the person who is asking us to do something for them doesn't like or respect us, that is likely to make us less willing to go the extra mile for them.

For example, have you noticed that when you like a person, if they make a mistake or do something wrong you will find excuses for them, but if someone you dislike does the same thing you will be metaphorically rubbing your hands with glee? That doesn't make us nasty – it just makes us human.

It is similar to when you buy a car and suddenly you notice all the other cars on the road that are the same as yours. We become highly attuned to those things that we are subconsciously 'looking' for. So, for example, with a person we don't like, we will notice all the things about them that confirm our dislike and ignore or disregard those things that contradict this feeling. We don't actively seek out people who *like* the object of our disdain. We're not really interested in hearing the contrary view – and we will tend to assume that those people are misguided or don't know how truly awful that person is!

Very few people wake up and think that they themselves are horrible people, even if we think they are. Most people wake up feeling pretty OK and justified in what they do and think most of the time. So telling someone they are horrid is highly unlikely to work. We don't believe it about ourselves so why should we believe it when other people say it? That is why it is so important to separate people's behaviour from who they are when we are dealing with them.

I think human beings are a bit like onions, made up of different layers. And if we understand that we cannot see inside but are only judging by the behaviour we observe, it might help us to stop making assumptions about others.

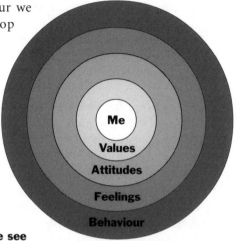

Me	– my core
Values	– what I am taught
Attitudes	– how my values affect my outlook
Feelings	– my emotional reaction
Behaviour	– what I do, what people see

The human onion

> **Me**

There is a central core, probably biologically based, which informs our general character. For example, if we are born with high levels of testosterone we are likely to be more adventurous as a child. If we have low levels of testosterone we are likely to be more cautious. However, even this innate bit is affected by what then happens to us as we grow up.

> **Values/Beliefs**

Our values are taught to us throughout our lives, but we are most sensitive to them when we are very young. We learn our values both formally and informally. For example, if we are brought up within a practising religion we will be formally told what we should believe about the world. However, and often more powerfully, we also learn our values from observing what others do – in particular, we learn a lot from observing our peers.

Example:
Value: Boys shouldn't cry

Attitudes

Our attitude to any situation we are in stems from our values. We will observe something happening, connect it to our value base (all subconsciously), and that will affect what we think about what we see.

Example:
Value: Boys shouldn't cry
Attitude: Boys who cry are weak

Feelings

Our feelings are influenced by our values and attitudes. We will have an emotional response to what we observe: a positive one if the environment or situation we are in is affirming our values and attitudes, and a negative one if they are challenging them.

Example:
Value: Boys shouldn't cry
Attitude: Boys who cry are weak
Situation: *A man crying at work*
Feeling: Uncomfortable, contemptuous

Behaviour

Our behaviour is informed by our response to our emotional stimuli, i.e. how we feel about the situation we are in. This is a part of the human onion that we can consciously control. If we are aware of our own personal biases and prejudices we might choose not to behave in a certain way, regardless of how we feel. For example, we can feel angry and act calmly, or feel nervous and act confidently. However, most often what happens is our feelings directly lead to our behaviour without conscious thought.

Example:
Value: Boys shouldn't cry
Attitude: Boys who cry are weak
Situation: *A man crying at work*
Feeling: Uncomfortable, contemptuous
Behaviour: Mock or walk away

What is most important to remember about the human onion is that actually you cannot always tell what someone's inner values, attitudes and feelings are simply by observing their behaviour. All people are different – a certain value does not automatically result in a certain behaviour. A lot also depends on the environment, personal awareness and self-control.

The seven factors

Over the years, as I've been thinking about what makes people tick, I have concluded that there are at least seven factors which influence the externally observed behaviours of a human being – which is probably why it is so difficult to understand or predict what and why people do what they do!

Factor 1 – biology

Our biology is determined primarily by our genes and the hormones to which we are exposed in our mother's womb. This has an influence on how our brain is constructed and programmes some of our genes to be predisposed to certain influences (e.g. extra testosterone in the womb may predispose us to be more of a risk-taker).

Factor 2 – age

As we grow older we begin to learn cultural and societal norms and either reject or accept them. For example, when I was a teenager drug-taking was considered a terrible social taboo, and those who took them were either radical extremists or dangerously experimental. This is not the case for many teenagers today, who cannot understand why those of us who come from a different 'time' are so 'uptight' about it.

Factor 3 – environment

This is what influences our growth and development, both physically and mentally. Does our diet make us fat, which influences how we see ourselves and how others see us? How many siblings do we have and how does that influence our sense of importance or control? Are we used to lots of unconditional love and support which promote our self-esteem or are we frequently criticised and put down?

Factor 4 – experience

Our own unique and personal experiences will inform our learning and affect how we are likely to perceive and respond to events in the future. For example, if we do well in public speaking at school, we are likely to be confident about speaking publicly in the future. If our first outing during school assembly was a disaster and resulted in sniggers and mocking from our schoolmates we are likely to view any form of public speaking in the future with fear and worry.

Factor 5 – understanding

Our own ability to analyse and reflect on our experiences will help to inform our thinking. The more we think about what we do the more control we have over what we do in the future. For example, if we are aware that our blood-sugar levels are low and that is likely to make us 'crabby' we may choose not to manifest our crabbiness in our behaviour (or go and eat something so that we don't feel crabby any more!).

Factor 6 – culture/society

The particular culture that we are immersed in and the societal norms that we are taught will influence how we behave. For example, Japanese culture very much emphasises respect for elders, deferring to their knowledge and experience. The American culture emphasises respect and autonomy for oneself. And of course there are sub-cultures such as religion, class, ethnic background and education which may influence how we see ourselves and how we view others who have different backgrounds to us.

Factor 7 – opportunities

These are the opportunities that we are faced with during our lives, which we either deal with well or badly and which influence how much we are driven by unconscious instinct and how much by conscious analysis. For example, if we are rejected from the school football team, dealing with it well will make it easier for us to deal with rejection in the future.

Assumptions

We tend to be attracted to people who are attracted to us. And we make massive assumptions about people based on how they look and sound.

For example, if someone speaks with what is regarded as a 'posh' accent, many of us will automatically make assumptions about who they are, where they were educated and what their values and aspirations are. If we share those values and aspirations we are likely to view them favourably. If we don't, we probably won't. But judging people purely on how they speak gives us no idea whatsoever about what sort of human being they are, so we need to learn not to make assumptions.

Before you start thinking, 'Oh, for goodness sake, Debra, we don't have to be saints!', I just want to make a point. If you don't think about why you dislike someone and what is going on for you internally in terms of your values, attitudes and feelings, you will never be able to win that person over. If you don't care about whether you win them over, then fine. But if you want to develop a better working relationship, you will need to test your assumptions about that individual.

So why do we make assumptions? Well, it's back to evolutionary psychology for this one. There are so many stimuli in the world that the brain has had to learn to simplify all the sensory inputs as quickly as possible so that we have time to react. For example, our ancestors didn't have time to see a bear running towards them and consider the motivations of the bear. Our brain is programmed 'BEAR. DANGEROUS. RUN'. Our brains are organised deliberately to take the minimum amount of information from a situation, compare that information with what we already know and make very rapid decisions. Therefore, it's daft to say to people, 'Don't make assumptions'. It is probably physically impossible to undo millennia of hard-wiring. But what we can do is be aware that we are automatically making assumptions about people and that those assumptions may well be wrong or based on erroneous interpretation of information.

What is the best way of managing this? Well, you need to consider your own value base. What assumptions are you making? You must really test your own thinking about the world and how you view those people who don't think the same way that you do. And you need to recognise that not everyone thinks in the same way that you do about every situation. Just because you see the world in a certain way, doesn't mean that others will.

Therefore, to deal with assumptions:

- Recognise that your first impression may be based on your prejudice or bias, not the reality. (By the way, for clarification, prejudice means that you are 'against' something and bias is when you are 'for' something. So, for example, you may be prejudiced against people who wear socks with sandals or biased towards people with brown eyes.)
- Actively listen to them – that means hearing what they are saying from their point of view, not yours
- Assume that your stereotype is wrong and test it
- Be aware that people behave differently in different situations, just as you do
- Don't look favourably on people just because they are like you, and vice versa
- Treat your positive and negative feelings about an individual with equal scepticism
- Don't judge others' behaviour by your own standards

Critically, to understand other human beings in their own unique context we have to switch off, as far as we possibly can, our own assumptions about them based on how they look, how they sound or how we are interpreting what they are saying. The fact is we all have our biases and prejudices. We are taught them from a very early age and even if we are aware of them, the basis of them is usually lost in the mist of childhood. It is practically impossible to rid ourselves of all our prejudices. However, what we can do is recognise that our instinctive reaction may well be born out of prejudice, and put it to one side.

It is intelligent to consider our internal responses to other human beings before we make conscious decisions about how we propose to interact with them. We need to try first to understand before attempting to be understood. We all see things in different ways – both physically and mentally – and the world can be confusing.

Consider the following image:

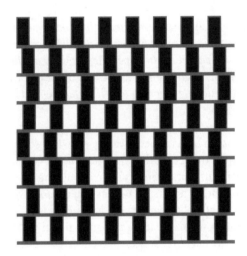

Are the horizontal lines parallel or do they slope?

In fact the lines are parallel. They don't slope at all. Our eyes are deceived by the way in which the black and white squares are spaced, forcing us to see the lines as sloped. This is how our eyes are programmed to work and we can't undo it. But we can recognise that simply because the lines look sloped and it is hard for us to see them as parallel, we can know that they are parallel and act accordingly.

Kidding ourselves

There is a theory of self-deception by a psychologist called Robert Trivers which essentially proposes that the human mind will convince itself of a different truth to the one that actually motivated us in the first place. In other words, we believe our own lies – they are not in fact lies to us at all. You will see this in action when you hear people swear blind that a certain thing didn't happen even when the evidence is before their own eyes. You may have seen or heard of the famous experiment where a group of people was shown a video of people dancing and moving about. For a very brief instant a man in a gorilla suit appears in the crowd and then disappears. Most people don't notice it because they are concentrating on the deliberate misdirection of the psychologist conducting the experiment. When they are shown it, some people laugh and accept that they missed it. But there are others who absolutely refuse to believe it and believe that the video was tampered with afterwards.

Stephen Pinker, in his excellent book *How the Mind Works*, talks about how *'our confabulations, not coincidentally, present us in the best light'.*[3] We want to feel good about ourselves and we will work very hard to recast our motivations in a positive light – and then believe that was what we had intended in the first place. As Pinker says:

> *More generally, we delude ourselves about how benevolent and how effective we are, a combination that social psychologists call benefectance. When subjects play games that are rigged by the experimenter, they attribute their successes to their own skill and their failures to the luck of the draw … For example, a person will recall enjoying a boring task if he had agreed to recommend it to others for paltry pay …*

What this means for us is that if we are viewing someone with dislike or suspicion we will hear things in what they say that fit our self-delusion and not what they actually mean. For example, if we are feeling vulnerable and our boss says to us 'Well, you didn't do that as well as you could have done', what we may convince ourselves we actually heard was, 'That simply wasn't good enough, you're rubbish at your job'. If we are hearing it from a position of emotional strength we are more likely to hear the subtext, 'Well, it was OK, but I think you are capable of more', meaning they think we are good at our job.

This is one of the reasons why it is almost pointless to argue logically with someone that their recall of a certain event is flawed – particularly when we discuss their motivation. The individual who tells tales on us to the boss may indeed have originally been motivated by spite, but the human desire to feel good about ourselves is so strong that they will quickly convince themselves, *and believe*, that their motivation was actually for the good of the organisation or team.

And this is true for you too. We all have our own little 'adoring mothers' at the back of our minds, convincing us that we are good people who don't do bad things deliberately. The reality is:

- We are good people
- We sometimes do bad things deliberately
- We will very quickly rewrite our motivation in our heads to convince ourselves that even if we can see what we did was bad, our motives were good

---

[3] Stephen Pinker (1997), *How the Mind Works*, Penguin, pp. 421–424.

The truth is that few of us are truly malicious. So it is important not to completely write off someone's character because they have done some things that are upsetting to us. You have probably upset some people in the past, either wittingly or unwittingly – and you would want people to 'forgive' you. No doubt Stephen Pinker would remind me that many of you reading this will convince yourselves that *your* motives are always completely good and pure and that I am wrong about you. That's OK – I think I'm a saint too!

REMEMBER:

- There are no simple 'causes' of human behaviour – there are many variables which affect how we think and behave and we are not necessarily in conscious control of them
- Separate people's behaviour from who they are
- Test your assumptions about people
- You may be deluding yourself about your motives
- You may be misinterpreting the motives of others

---

2 It's all in your head

The brain is a wonderful organ. It starts working when you get up in the morning and doesn't stop until you get to the office.
Robert Frost, US poet (1874–1963)

Outcomes

After reading this chapter you will:
- Have a very basic understanding of the structure and workings of the human brain
- Understand how our brains have evolved to produce the behaviours we see today
- Understand that brain structure, chemicals and processes can influence our emotional states

Any discussion about human beings interacting with one another cannot be complete without an understanding of how our brains function physically and how the physical structures and processes in the brain affect how we think about and act around other people. However, it is important to make a distinction here. Though we have a lot of information about how the brain works, we have very little information about how the mind works. We know what physical structures and systems exist and largely what they are involved in. We know, for example, that neurons use electrical signals to pass chemicals (hormones, in fact) between them in order to start a new electrical signal. What we're not clear about is how this process affects how we think and feel – the brain can be thought of as the physical structure and processes of biology, but the mind is the 'outcome' of those physical structures and processes, i.e. our psychology.

So the truth is that we do not really know how our minds (our conscious experiences and processes) work even though we know a lot about the biology of the brain. Understanding how the brain works can at best give us some insight into how human beings think and react. But human experience and emotion probably cannot be reduced to pure empirical data.

If you are not particularly interested in this topic then you can skip this chapter and still gain from the book. However, reading it should make your understanding of yourself and others richer and more rewarding. It also gives some context for what can often appear to be the completely illogical actions of others.

It is worth pointing out that the human brain, both biologically (its make-up and structures) and psychologically (emotions, motivations and consciousness), is a vast and complex subject, large parts of which remain to be analysed and understood. Those of you who have studied this will know that inevitably, therefore, genuine scientific explanations are a great deal more complex than the way in which I am able to describe them in this chapter. Those of you who are experts, forgive me – I have necessarily kept my explanations as simple as is reasonably possible, hopefully giving enough information to explain in broad terms what is happening and perhaps motivating some of you to find out more about this fascinating subject.

The structure of the human brain

Evidence shows that there is a link between the structures of our brains and how we interact with one another in a social setting. This is why, in my view, it is helpful to have some understanding of what the brain looks like and what it does.

In very simple terms the brain does three major things:
1. Analyses sensory stimuli (a sound, a look, a smell)
2. Elicits a response to that stimuli
3. Provides motivation, i.e. decides to act on the stimuli

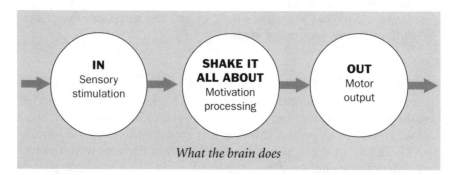

What the brain does

What many people aren't aware of is that the spinal cord is also an extension of the brain. In fact, in mammalian development the brain essentially 'grew out' of the spinal cord. The spinal cord itself is made up of grey matter (cell bodies) and white matter (nerve fibres), just like the brain. Most sensory information (with the exception of sight and hearing) travels to the spinal cord via skin and internal organs. These often share the same neurons (the cells which process and pass on information) which is why, for example, sensory information from the heart uses the same neurons as sensory information from the left shoulder and why pain in the left shoulder can be a sign of a heart attack. Most reflexes occur in the spinal cord.

There are essentially four main parts to the brain: the frontal lobe is where thinking, planning and cognition (information processing) happens; the parietal lobe houses the somatosensory cortex and processes sensations; the occipital lobe is where vision is processed; and the temporal lobe controls hearing.

Having said this I need to add a note of caution. As Susan Greenfield says, '*We now know, thanks both to clinical observation and to neuroscientific research, that* there is no simple one-to-one matching between a function and a particular part of the brain.'[1]

The cerebral cortex is the term used to describe the 'outside' part of the brain, which is where sensory information is analysed, in particular vision, touch, hearing and the co-ordination of motor responses (i.e. muscle movements).

One of the most interesting facts about how the brain works is that for motor activities (that is the brain sending messages to your muscles to make them move) there are very specific regions of the brain dedicated to them. For example, the cross-section below shows which parts of the brain typically control key parts of our bodies.

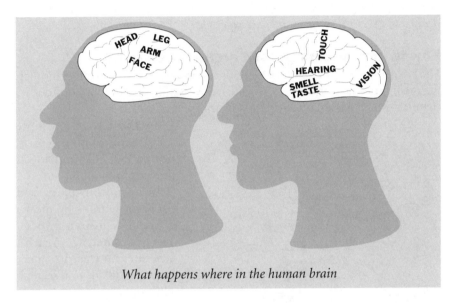

What happens where in the human brain

What is interesting is that research by neuroscientists (who study the way the structure of the brain affects human behaviour) shows that for social interactions involving thinking about other human beings there is no specific associated brain region. In fact activity in one part of the brain can create a ripple effect, so if you observe in MRI scans what is going on in the brain during social situations you will see oscillating waves of neurons 'lighting up' over various parts of the brain.

The association cortex is the bit of the brain that compares information from memory with primary sensory information to provide context and meaning. These areas are called areas of 'higher' processing. This is because they do not receive direct input from the senses nor do they send direct signals to organise motor responses. It is this part of the brain which determines your personality traits; your decision making and your voluntary activity (i.e. consciously deciding to smile as opposed to reflexively smiling).

The hippocampus is buried deep in the brain. This plays a role in contextualising sensory experiences in terms of past experiences. It has strong

---

[1] Susan Greenfield (2000), *The Private Life of the Brain*, Allen Lane/Penguin Press, p. 6.

links with those parts of the brain that are involved in motivational and emotional responses. This forms part of something you are probably familiar with: the limbic system.

Broadly speaking, the limbic system is the term used to describe the structures in the brain that influence emotion, motivation and the link between emotion and memory. The hippocampus, the amygdala and the hypothalamus are some of the many discrete structures that contribute to this system.

The limbic system and the association cortex are very closely linked and allow human beings to make conscious decisions about emotional and sensory inputs.

'While the cerebral cortex is involved in the analysis of sensory stimuli and the direction of motor commands, the limbic system provides the emotional responses, the link with deeper feelings and past experience.'[2]

How is information passed around the brain?

The brain is made up of neurons. Neurons communicate with each other through the medium of neurotransmitters, which are essentially a kind of hormone or chemical which passes information between parts of the brain.

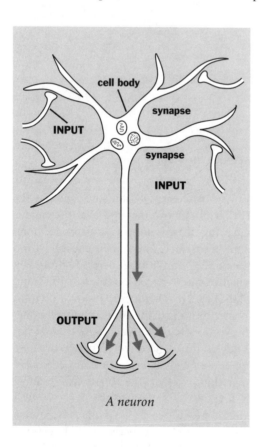

A neuron

To the left is a simple picture of what a typical neuron looks like and how it passes information.

Information is passed between neurons by means of these neurotransmitters. The originating neuron generates an electric signal, lasting 1/1000th of a second. This signal races at around 250 mph to the point on the neuron which stores the transmitter. The electric signal essentially allows the transmitters to be released into the synapse (the gap between the neurons). Each transmitter has a particular shape and when it travels across the gap it slots into the appropriate shape on the other neuron (called the receptor). This generates a new electrical signal … and so the process goes on.

[2] David Robinson (ed.) (1998), *Neurobiology (Biology: Brain & Behaviour, 2)*, Springer-Verlag/ Open University Press, p. 186.

Neurons communicating

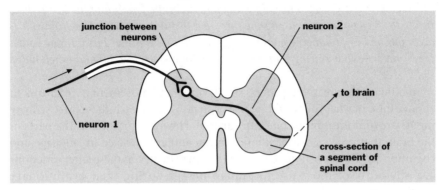

The brain contains something in the region of 100 billion neurons and there are approximately 100 trillion interconnections between them. That's a lot of activity! And that is also why the surface of the brain looks a bit like a desiccated prune – it's only by this folding and creasing that enough space is created for all of these neurons to exist.

Interestingly, neurotransmitters don't just exist in the brain. For example, serotonin is a type of neurotransmitter involved in mood. More than 90 per cent of all the serotonin in the body actually resides in the gut. This is one of the reasons why emotional experiences often have physical manifestations in other parts of our body and probably where the expression 'gut instinct' comes from.

Susan Greenfield compares the brain to a large city like New York. Each neuron represents a room in the city, while people living there are like the neurotransmitters: some sedentary, some rushing about, some staying in the local area, some spreading far away from their 'home'.

So why does all this matter? Well, because people's moods, behaviours and reactions can be hugely affected by the type and quantity of these transmitters in the brain. For example, noradrenaline is the transmitter that causes human beings to prepare their bodies for flight or fight. In the brain, it is involved in many aspects of brain function and is important in the development of the visual system. Over-stimulation of noradrenaline receptors is linked to feeding and drinking behaviours and symptoms of mania.

Another neurotransmitter is Acetylcholine (Ach), which was the very first neurotransmitter to be discovered. Its release from neurons impacts on arousal, motivation and emotion. There is also evidence to link it to learning and memory processes.

Evolutionary psychology

Evolutionary psychology is the study of how our brains have evolved over time to make us behave in the ways that we currently do.

Studies comparing primate brains with our own show how the human brain diverged from our common ancestor to develop bigger and more specialised areas in response to our changing environment and therefore our changing behaviour. As Stephen Pinker says, '... *the primate brain must have been considerably re-engineered to end up as a human brain. Our brains are about three times too big for a generic monkey or ape of our body size. The inflation is accomplished by prolonging fetal brain growth for a year after birth. If our bodies grew proportionally during that period, we would be ten feet tall and weigh half a ton.*'[3]

In humans the areas that process smell, vision and movement have shrunk to about a third of what you would see in a primate, where clearly these three sensory inputs are of critical importance in survival. However, in humans the parts of the brain that process complex information and are involved in language and cognition are disproportionately larger than in primates, as these latter functions are obviously of more use to human beings during their evolutionary development.

The good news
There is a great deal of evidence to demonstrate that we have, in fact, evolved to be loving, caring and empathetic, not just towards our immediate family and friends but also towards others. There is a common misconception that human beings are innately designed to be selfish. This is largely due to a complete misunderstanding of Richard Dawkins's work on evolution and in particular his coining of the term 'the selfish gene'. Dawkins never said that human beings have evolved to be selfish – his work related to the actions of genes, not people! (Note: don't take what you read in the media at face value and beware those people who espouse opinions about others' work if they haven't read the original text! If you want to be sure of your facts, my advice is to go to the source.)

Neuroscientists have discovered a thing called 'primal empathy'.[4] Basically this is an innate human ability to sense the emotional state of another instantaneously. This can happen even if the person we are with is not speaking. Our ability subconsciously and rapidly to assess the emotional state of another is mostly based on our interpretation of the non-verbal signals that are being given: the look in the eyes; a fleeting downturn of the mouth; a brief tensing of the facial muscles. All these are clues that are being unconsciously processed (largely in the hippocampus and the rest of the limbic system) but that are nonetheless triggering activity in our brains, which leads us to make more conscious assessments about the person we are with (via the association cortex).

The bad news
The bad news is that this part of our brains (the orbitofrontal cortex) also makes us react at a deep level to what we are observing in another human being and unless we are able to bring that deep unconscious reaction into our consciousness we will be unable to unpack our emotional responses and think about the context in which we are receiving this information. This limits our ability to choose how to act. This means that there is a danger that we will respond to this very primitive

[3] Stephen Pinker (1997), *How the Mind Works*, Penguin, pp. 183–184.
[4] Daniel Goleman (2006), *Social Intelligence*, Hutchinson.

ancient system in a way that may not be appropriate in the moment or that may not help us to achieve what we are trying to achieve. Our association cortex has either not kicked in or is being overwhelmed by the sensory input and emotional context.

The neuroscientist Joseph LeDoux found that fear is controlled in two different ways in the brain. The first way takes what he calls the 'low road': that is, we react instinctively and intuitively to the 'danger' without considering the realities or the consequences. The second way he calls the 'high road': here, the information is processed by the orbitofrontal or sensory cortex and although this makes reactions slower it means that we are less likely to make mistakes. Of course, 'slower' in this context means milliseconds, not hours!

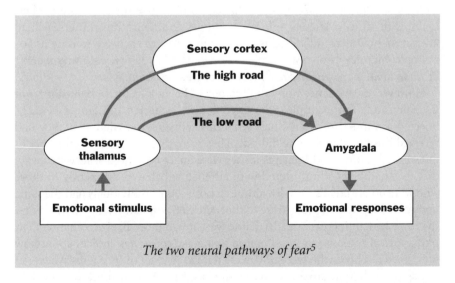

The two neural pathways of fear[5]

In terms of social interactions, there are no specific areas of the brain linked to decisions about, for example, how to respond to people, how to interpret social situations and so on. Nature is very clever and very economical. It is highly likely that, as our human bodies evolved in response to our environment and we needed

[5] Joseph LeDoux (2004), *The Emotional Brain: The Mysterious Underpinnings of Emotional Life*, Phoenix Press.

to form relationships and social bonds to ensure our survival, nature simply adapted existing neurological pathways. The result of this is that processing of social information happens over a number of parts of the brain – sometimes simultaneously. Thus the brain operates like a sort of network.

This orbitofrontal cortex is connected to the association cortex, the limbic system and the spine via the brain stem. Information is passed and processed extremely rapidly between these systems. Thus, information and the processing of it is co-ordinated almost instantaneously and is what enables us to make quick, on-the-spot decisions about how to respond to the social situation and the emotional context we are in, such as stooping to hug a crying child, raising our voice to a rude queue-breaker or smiling back at a smiling stranger. In fact, these connections are so fast that sometimes we think we are acting spontaneously when in fact it is just that our decisions have been made so fast we are unaware that we are deciding!

Emotions – genes or choice?

Nature is often hidden, sometimes overcome, seldom extinguished.

Francis Bacon

From a biological perspective there is overwhelming evidence to show that the fundamental structural formation of a human being is through their genes. These genes create an individual physiology which the individual then uses to interact with the world. Their size, weight, shape and of course the structure of their brain, with all its particular mix of hormones and neurotransmitters, will all impact on how that individual is able to interact with their environment. For example, high levels of testosterone *'sensitise nervous system pathways making the individual more sensitive to ... erotic thoughts and stimuli'*.[6]

However, the evidence points to biology as being a factor in behaviour, not the sole cause. For example, two psychologists, Schacter and Singer (1962),[7] injected a number of individuals with adrenaline; some knew that they had received this boost and some did not. They were then exposed to a number of different situations and their responses were analysed. Those who were aware that they had been administered with adrenaline behaved differently to those who were not aware. Essentially, although both sets of individuals had the same bodily reaction to situations (due to the increased adrenaline), those who knew that they had an increase in adrenaline were much more likely to analyse their physiological response to the situation and make conscious choices about how they reacted. Those who were not aware tended to react more aggressively.

Based on that argument, it makes much more sense to think of a gene as predisposing a person to a particular type of situation or influence. If individuals are aware of how they are likely to respond emotionally and physically, they have the opportunity to make conscious choices about how to react.

---

[6] Richard Stevens (1996), *Understanding the Self*, Sage Publications, pp. 40.

[7] Stanley Schachter and Jerome E. Singer (1962), *Cognitive, Social and Physiological Determinants of Emotional State*.

Fritjof Capra points to evidence that *'Peptides [hormones that operate in the gut as well as the brain] are the biochemical manifestation of the emotions ... they interlink and integrate mental, emotional and biological activities'.*[8] Thus, as we have seen, emotions are not just a social or mental construct. They are a biological reality. In other words, our bodies are programmed to experience emotion physically, hence we feel sick when we are nervous, our hearts pound when we are angry and our palms sweat when we are in love.

However, understanding how your body and brain react to certain stimuli can help you to make conscious choices about what you do. We will explore our conscious choices in the rest of the book.

REMEMBER:

- Our genes only predispose us to certain behaviour – they are not a guarantee of it
- The human brain has a basic emotional response mechanism – and a higher functioning conscious choice mechanism
- Our emotions are 'hard-wired' into our brains by millennia of evolutionary drivers
- We have evolved to be loving, caring and empathetic
- Knowing how our brains and bodies are contributing to our emotional state can help us to make a choice about how to respond in a given situation

[8] Fritjof Capra (1997), *The Web of Life: A New Scientific Understanding of Living Systems*, Anchor, p. 283.

3 Learning to listen

There are twelve pots of honey in my cupboard and they've been calling me for hours. I couldn't hear them properly because Rabbit would keep talking, but if nobody says anything except those twelve pots, then I shall know where they're coming from.
Winnie the Pooh, A. A. Milne

Outcomes

After reading this chapter you will:
- **Know how 'natural' listening occurs**
- **Know your own communication style and how it can impact on others**
- **Know how to adapt your style to be more effective in your communications**

Listening

It's a funny thing; we are taught how to speak, how to write and how to read. Yet the most important communication skill of all – listening – we are left to pick up on our own. It's no surprise, then, that so many of us are really not as good at listening as we purport to be.

The ability really to listen is at the heart of all communication and all studies of communication, coaching and mentoring strategies. But it's not that easy to do. The problem is that we have all sorts of interfering thoughts that run through our heads while we are listening.

First, there is a thing called the listening process. An individual begins to speak and eventually makes their point. Some people take a long time to get to the point – but there's usually one in there somewhere! What usually happens is that we listen to the first part of what they have to say, and then we begin mentally to prepare a response. This can simply involve accessing information in our own heads that agrees or disagrees with the speaker, or the speaker has said something that has sent the mind wandering off down a different thought route, or we have assumed that we know what the point is going to be. This is when interruption happens. Not necessarily physical interruption, i.e. opening our mouths and cutting across the speaker, but sometimes simply mental interruption – we just stop listening, without realising it. I'm sure you have noticed it in yourselves sometimes: we find ourselves suddenly tuning back in to a conversation without even being aware that we had left it in the first place!

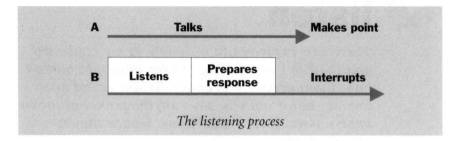

The listening process

The listening process I describe happens to all of us much of the time, usually unconsciously. So when we are communicating we need to bear in mind that neither we nor our listener are listening with full attention. However, there are a number of ways to combat this if you are the speaker:

- Get to the point quickly – don't pad out what you are saying with unnecessary detail
- Repeat the key points that you want the listener to understand and remember
- Ask the listener questions to ensure they have understood. (However, don't say, 'Have you understood?'. Unfortunately, people will nearly always say that they have – and not because they are telling fibs but because they genuinely believe that they have even if they haven't!)

How we listen
When we listen we are listening through a filter of our mental map of the world. This can be broken down into the 'six Es'.

The six Es

Ears	**The actual words we hear and the tone in which they are expressed**
	But mostly we will pay attention to the tone of voice in which the words are spoken – and that is what will give us the message. If someone says in a voice of doom and gloom,'This project will be challenging', we will hear it negatively. If they say it in an upbeat chirpy tone, people will hear it positively. The actual words themselves are not what give the message.
Eyes	**The body language we observe**
	Much like tone, the real message is given through body language. If someone is frowning slouching and generally looking defeated when they say, 'This project is challenging', then we will assume the project will be too difficult to achieve. If, however, they are smiling, standing upright and looking enthusiastic, then we will assume the project is going to be fun.

Experience	**What has happened to us in the past** *We filter all of our listening through our own experiences. If we have participated in this type of project before and it's always gone wrong then that experience will colour how we hear the project being introduced to us.*
Emotions	**How we are feeling** *There are two elements to this: pre-emotional state and post-emotional state. The pre-emotional state is how we are feeling at the start of the communication. If we are already feeling negative or low then that will be a powerful filter through which we hear any messages given. The post-emotional state is how we feel during the message – if, for example, a particular word is used which upsets us then that emotion will affect the rest of what we hear*
Expectation	**What we think will happen/we will hear** *Based on our emotional states and our experiences before the speaker has finished speaking (and sometimes before they have begun, if we have a particular opinion about that speaker), we will already be expecting a certain outcome.*
Egos	**Wanting to feel good about ourselves** *In a room full of noise where it is difficult to pick out any one particular sentence it's amazing how we will immediately hear if someone mentions our name! We are highly attuned to those things that are directly relevant to us. So when we are listening we will be subconsciously but nonetheless actively listening for those things that either reinforce our sense of self-esteem or in some way demean it. We will notice and pick up on those words and tones more than anything else and may often miss other salient information because of that.*

So when you are listening, concentrate on those things that will help you to understand what the speaker is saying.

The following are the types of listening that limit our effectiveness in communicating with others:

- Listening for me being right
- Listening for an opportunity to punish
- Listening for proving I know best
- Listening for making my point
- Listening for letting off steam
- Listening for telling my story
- Listening for you being wrong

The following are the types of listening that will make us more effective as communicators:

- Listening to try to understand
- Listening for a way to solve a problem
- Listening for possible action

- Listening for new possibilities
- Listening for a way to resolving breakdowns
- Listening for a way to build relationships

Communication styles

Remember that everyone's listening is imperfect and that you will be listening to others with the six Es and they will be listening to you in the same way. However, knowing your own communication style can help you to adapt your speaking to the other person's listening, which gives you a better chance of being understood. It also means that your understanding may improve if you are aware of how your style may differ to someone else's.

Communication-style test

I invented the following communication-style test as a way of helping people to understand how different communication styles can result in misunderstandings. It is not scientifically validated and you can cheat! I want you to see it simply as a tool to help you to communicate more effectively.

Instructions

Look at one row at a time. Give each word a value from **1** to **4**, with **4** representing the word most like you and **1** representing the word least like you. You must have one of each number only in every row so that each row adds up to **10**. In other words every line must contain a **4**, a **3**, a **2** and a **1**.

Example

Funny	4	Interesting	2	Quiet	1	Determined	3

The test

Accurate		Patient		Friendly		Direct	
Adventurous		Systematic		Loyal		Persuasive	
Impulsive		Stubborn		Judgemental		Passive	
Neighbourly		Confident		Self-reliant		Competent	
Forceful		Optimistic		Gentle		Conventional	
Colourful		Even-tempered		Restrained		Quick	
Predictable		Practical		Outspoken		Emotional	
Perfectionist		Impatient		Talkative		Gullible	
Good listener		Law-abiding		Self-directed		High-spirited	
Playful		Risk-taker		Cautious		Content	

Copy your score from the original sheet on to this one.

Accurate		Patient		Friendly		Direct	
Adventurous		Systematic		Loyal		Persuasive	
Impulsive		Stubborn		Judgemental		Passive	
Neighbourly		Confident		Self-reliant		Competent	
Forceful		Optimistic		Gentle		Conventional	
Colourful		Even-tempered		Restrained		Quick	
Predictable		Practical		Outspoken		Emotional	
Perfectionist		Impatient		Talkative		Gullible	
Good listener		Law-abiding		Self-directed		High-spirited	
Playful		Risk-taker		Cautious		Content	

Scoring the communication-style test

Now add up your scores for each colour and mark them against the boxes below.

GREEN			BLUE	
YELLOW			RED	

Explanations of communication-style test

You will find that you have different scores in each of the boxes. Some of you will find you have scored very highly in one or two areas and less in others. And some of you will find that you have a relatively even spread of scores. There is no right or wrong spread of scores. Good communication is actually not about you – it's about how your style differs from others and your ability to adjust your style to your listener.

If you scored highly on '**green**' then it means that you are largely facts-led in your communication style. You are interested in evidence and information. You will communicate by sharing facts and you will listen out for facts and evidence.

If you scored highly on '**blue**' it means you are largely feelings-led in your communication style. You are interested in emotions and how people feel about things. You will focus on these things when you speak and will look out for them when you listen.

If you scored highly on '**yellow**' it means you are largely influenced by creative possibilities and ideas in your communication style. You will focus on what is new and different when you communicate and you will listen out for fun and ideas when you are the listener.

If you scored highly on '**red**' it means you are largely influenced by practical action and results. You will be interested in what can be done about something, what the immediate action or results might be. These words will feature heavily in your own speaking and you will be highly attuned to them in someone else's speaking.

As I said earlier – none of these are the right way to communicate. It is just that it is possible that we will perceive those people who do not communicate in the same way that we do in a negative fashion. We will not necessarily hear them in the way they intended.

Perceptions

The point behind this test is that when we are listening to people we will be 'perceiving' where they are coming from through our own preferred style. If we are action orientated and find detail distracting, then we are likely to find those people who want to explore all the possible ramifications of a decision as difficult and using delaying tactics. The point is that they are not being deliberately difficult or delaying, it's just that the way in which they process and use communication and information is very different to yours. And guess what? They will have a similarly negative view of you.

So it is important to recognise that your interpretation of someone's communication or their response to yours is not about reality – it's almost solely about your perception.

We will have negative and positive views about people based on their communication styles and it is important to be aware of how those views might inadvertently 'prejudice' or 'bias' us against or towards a particular individual.

Possible perceptions of communication styles

	Positive perceptions	Negative perceptions
GREEN **Facts-led**	■ Practical ■ Pays attention to details ■ Gets the facts right ■ Makes clear, logical decisions ■ Authoritative ■ Takes time to think	■ Too much order ■ Over attention to detail ■ Never gets anything done ■ Always plays by the rules ■ Closed minded ■ Overly focused on facts
BLUE **Feelings-led**	■ Caring ■ Supportive ■ Interested in individuals ■ Nurturing ■ Cares about relationships ■ Warm ■ Good listener	■ Over-nurturing ■ Misplaced loyalties ■ Puts individuals over the task ■ Doesn't let people grow or make their own mistakes ■ Hangs on to poor performers ■ Too soft

YELLOW **Ideas-led**	■ Enthusiastic ■ Creative – prepared to experiment ■ Fun to work with ■ Open minded ■ Ready to challenge the status quo ■ Looks for new possibilities	■ Addicted to change ■ Starts things and doesn't finish them ■ Has lots of initiatives all at once ■ Doesn't get results ■ Doesn't see things through

RED **Results-led**	■ Confident ■ Quick ■ Gets results ■ Dynamic ■ Focused ■ Inspiring	■ Action only ■ Not concerned about individuals ■ Doesn't listen well ■ Doesn't think things through ■ Not interested in detail

The point about all of this is that these are *only* perceptions – they are not necessarily true of the individual. If you want to communicate more effectively and build better relationships, understand that you may be seeing someone in a particular light simply because they have a different style to you.

About 15 years ago I used to work with a guy called Trevor. Trevor and I absolutely loathed one another. I thought he was a completely pompous prig and he thought I was a reckless upstart! We attended a training course together in which we did a similar exercise to the communication-style test I have shown you here. It turned out that he was completely green and I was completely red! Once we had realised that, actually, our motivations were the same, i.e. we both wanted to do our jobs well but we just went about it in different ways, it completely changed our relationship. We ended up getting on really well and went on *voluntarily* to work on some projects together!

The trick is to know how to adapt your style to suit others. You don't necessarily need to know precisely what their style is. They don't have to fill in a questionnaire – usually it is fairly obvious. Experiment with your communication approach until you find the one that works with that individual.

Suggested ways of dealing with different communication styles

	Characteristics	*Possible approaches*
GREEN **Facts-led**	■ Logical ■ Decides after evaluation ■ Wants appreciation for job done – but does not want to be condescended to ■ More concerned with ideas and principles than people ■ May be self-critical	■ Acknowledge skill ■ Present facts and information ■ Present ideas logically ■ Speak calmly ■ Avoid over-emotion ■ Focus on benefits
BLUE **Feelings-led**	■ Nice ■ Can be slow to change ■ Avoids confrontation and conflict ■ Wants harmony ■ Likes to know motivations ■ Intuitive	■ Take interest in them as people ■ Establish rapport ■ Speak calmly ■ Focus on people outcomes ■ Talk about 'gut' feelings ■ Explain the 'why'
YELLOW **Ideas-led**	■ Fun ■ Enthusiastic ■ Optimistic ■ Unstructured ■ Can be mischievous ■ Forms opinions from feelings ■ People oriented	■ Use humour ■ Talk about feelings ■ Be passionate ■ Focus on the positive ■ Explain the 'why' ■ Don't take topic too seriously
RED **Action-led**	■ Direct ■ Results oriented ■ Loves change and challenge ■ Decides quickly ■ Risk taker ■ Seeks solutions ■ Can be hasty	■ Be direct and to the point ■ Focus on the new and exciting ■ Mix facts and feelings ■ Focus on actions ■ Keep the hows/whys brief ■ Acknowledge desire for speedy results

The above characteristics and possible approaches are of course generalisations. All people are different and will have a mix of characteristics.

To sum up, this short chapter has concentrated very much on being clear about how you communicate and listen and how that can impact on those around you.

If you get the opportunity you could try suggesting to your colleagues that you all complete this questionnaire and see what happens. But I strongly suggest you don't complete it about each other. People have strong views about who they are and unless you are very skilled it could cause enormous hurt and damage if someone's self-view turns out to be very different to how you see them.

REMEMBER:

- **All of us struggle to listen well – be patient**
- **Our listening comes through filters that can distort what we are hearing**
- **Listen to understand**
- **Be clear about your own preferred communication style**
- **Adapt your style to the needs of your listener**

4 Walking in another man's moccasins

Humans have already changed the world several times by changing the way they have conversations.
Theodore Zeldin

Outcomes

After reading this chapter you will:
- **Understand that people have different mental constructs about the world**
- **Have a basic understanding of NLP techniques**
- **Be able to use NLP to broaden your communication skills**

Culture and context

You have probably noticed that the most socially adept people seem to recognise that they need to adapt how they communicate with others according to the culture and context they are in.

For example, if they see a child crying because she has fallen over and hurt herself they would be unlikely to stand over her and shout. They would probably lower themselves to her eye level, lower the tone of their voice and speak softly and kindly. If, however, they see one child deliberately hurting another they are likely to stand tall and raise their voice.

In fact, most of us subconsciously adapt our behaviour as a matter of course in normal circumstances, which means that most of us are probably fairly socially adept.

But those people who are truly good at communicating with others take it one step further. They consciously think about how to listen and interact with another person in context and take the other person's cultural norms into account.

Cultural norms can also be called 'social norms', that is those behaviours that are seen as acceptable by the particular society. A classic example is bowing to a Japanese person. The bow is seen as polite and socially acceptable. Bowing to an British person in greeting would be seen as odd and outside what is the normally accepted social norm.

Getting it wrong is extremely embarrassing! I remember a few years ago my then Deputy Chief Executive, Meena Varma, and I flew up to Edinburgh to meet the Chief Executive of a major Scottish voluntary organisation. We had never met him before, but of course we knew of him. When we arrived at his offices he came out to greet us. He bent slightly forward with his head while extending his hand. Unfortunately I completely misread what he was doing and assumed he was 'coming in' for an air kiss. I duly pursed my lips. However, what he was trying to do was shake my hand and our misunderstanding resulted in me accidentally kissing him on the lips! I can't speak for him but I was mortified when I realised what I had done. To make the situation worse, he then had to kiss Meena otherwise it would have looked even odder.

We generally don't kiss people we don't know on the lips – particularly in a professional situation! – and I think that that moment of misunderstanding manifested itself subtly and in other ways during our subsequent meeting. Needless to say it didn't go according to plan and I suspect it was as much to do with that social dissonance at the very beginning which put us all in an awkward position. We simply didn't manage to find much common ground after that, even though we did try. I wonder now if getting it so badly wrong at the beginning hampered our ability to communicate effectively and that may have been a key factor in what could have been a very powerful partnership between our two organisations never really taking off.

The point here is that it is easy to get it wrong. We misread signals; we hear what is being said through our own filters. But the fact is that people do have slightly different ways of looking at the world and we can help ourselves enormously if we understand that and, further, make the effort to understand *their* world.

This is fairly obvious when we are dealing with people from a different culture to ours. However, it is also true of people within our own culture and society and that is where we can so often get it horribly wrong.

NLP

There are many misunderstandings about what neuro-linguistic programming (NLP) is, largely because it's one of those topics that some unscrupulous people have latched on to without proper training. However, at its basis is a simple premise: people have different ways of looking at the world and if you want to be effective in interacting with them it helps if you can understand their way of thinking. This surely makes a lot of sense.

This chapter is not an introduction to the whole basis of NLP. I simply pick out some of the techniques NLP uses in the hope that you may find some of them work for you.

At its heart NLP is about understanding and interacting with others in a way that makes use of the fact that people see the world in different ways. There are so many sensory stimuli we receive from the world that our minds have to find a way of coping. One of the things NLP says is that what people do is build maps of their world and these maps produce filters though which we view our experiences. There is an Arabic saying: 'What a piece of bread looks like depends on whether you are hungry or not'.

There is a lot of detail involved in NLP studies, and more is added all the time as this is a developing discipline. I don't propose even to attempt to cover all of it here. I will simply pick out some of the principles and techniques in NLP that you should find relatively easy to apply in your dealings with people. These are techniques that I have used myself and have found work for the most part. But, be warned, it's not a science, it's an art and it is not *guaranteed* to work.

NLP says that people have a preference in the way in which they represent the world, both in how they experience it and how they 'explain' the experience to themselves: either visual, auditory or kinaesthetic. (There is also olfactory and gustatory – but for the purposes of this discussion we will concentrate on the common three.)

Visual people respond to visual signals and will visualise things. For example, commonly visual people will stare off into the distance while they are thinking or listening because they are picturing or visualising whatever it is you are discussing. If you are not a visual person yourself you may find this irritating or an indication that the individual is not paying you any attention, when in fact that is not the case. Auditory people concentrate on tone and words and will say things like 'I hear what you are saying' and 'it sounds like it might work'. Kinaesthetic people tend to be focusing on how they are feeling, both physically and emotionally, and will use terms like 'it doesn't feel right' or 'my gut instinct is'.

Of course, most of us all have these senses and therefore use them. But usually we will find that we have a preference for the way in which we represent our worlds, and mostly that will be either visually, auditory or kinaesthetically.

NLP argues that human beings will respond to different use of language. In simple terms visual people will respond better to pictures, diagrams, stories and models and will like the opportunity to visualise for themselves. Auditory people will respond better to powerful use of tone, words and sounds. Kinaesthetic people will respond better to stimuli that provoke feelings in them or where they can connect with the feelings of others. Of course, this is neither an exact science nor as polarised as I have described it here. However, it is useful to bear in mind when thinking about what makes human beings so different and yet so much the same.

In NLP terms it is relatively easy to find out quickly what kind of mental map the person you are communicating with has. This is because there are physical signs of what we are thinking about and how we are thinking, which are shown in the position of our eyes. NLP terms these lateral eye movements as 'eye accessing cues' because they are clues as to how the person is processing information.

The faces below are displayed as if you are looking at someone, so each left and right corresponds to your perspective, not theirs.

Visualisation
Eyes looking straight ahead/defocused/looking into the distance

Visual remembered images	**Visual constructed images**
(what we saw)	(what we imagine we saw)
Eyes to the upper right	Eyes to the upper left

Remembered sounds	**Constructed sounds**
(what we heard)	(what we imagine we heard)
Eyes to the centre right	Eyes to the centre left

Auditory digital	**Kinaesthetic**
(internal dialogue)	(feelings and bodily sensations)
Eyes to the lower right	Eyes to the lower left

Using the cues

With practice, noticing someone's eye movement can give you a fairly good indication as to whether they are visual, auditory or kinaesthetic. This can help you to use the kind of language that they best respond to in order for you to influence them. Below are some examples of phrases you can use to a) identify or confirm for yourself what kind of thinking the listener is engaging in and b) help them listen to what you have to say.

Visual phrases	Auditory phrases	Kinaesthetic phrases
I see what you mean	I hear what you say	I can grasp that idea
I am looking into it	Let me take a sounding	Let me sleep on it
We see eye to eye	Music to my ears	We have a connection
The future looks bright	It sounds really good	It feels great
I'll see you soon	Look forward to chatting soon	I'll get in touch with you soon
This should shed light on the matter	That rings a bell	I can grasp that idea
Show me what you mean	It's all Greek to me	I can't put my finger on it
Beyond a shadow of a doubt	Music to my ears	It feels right

Words and language

> *'When I use a word,' Humpty Dumpty said in a rather scornful tone, 'it means just what I choose it to mean – neither more nor less.' 'The question is,' said Alice, 'whether you can make words mean different things.' 'The question is,' said Humpty Dumpty, 'which is to be master – that's all.'*
>
> Lewis Carroll, *Alice in Wonderland*

The important message in NLP is that words do not have a meaning independent of the meaning that we assign to them or the context that they are in. Words are filtered differently depending upon the context and preferences of the person to whom we are talking. Let's take as an example a rose. All of us would agree that it is a flower. However, some of us might think of it as something beautiful and romantic, while others might think that it is sickly smelling and sets off their asthma. And this is where we can so often miscommunicate with people. We may say, 'You should sit down and relax' to someone who is just about to go off to the gym, but for them going to the gym may be a form of relaxation. For us relaxing might be vegging out in front of the TV and we would see going to the gym as hard work.

Generally, speakers have a fully thought out and complete idea of what they want to say to someone. This is called 'deep structure' by linguists. We are not always consciously aware of it but it exists nonetheless. However, it would be far too tedious, for both us and our listener, if we described the entire context of our thinking in our speaking (although this is a rather annoying trait that my mother, Louise, and I have in common, according to our partners! We have a tendency to give all the background, including the life histories of the protagonists in our particular story, what we were wearing, what they were wearing, how we're convinced that our partners have met them – '… *you remember, the guy with the goatee, wearing espadrilles of all things – in the middle of November for goodness sake! You made that comment about ageing hippies which nobody laughed at and you were really embarrassed … he had the wife with the rather unfortunate ears … we met them at the Reids' house when we had that delicious prawn dish … which I got the recipe for but when I cooked it something went wrong with the temperature setting on the oven (which you still haven't fixed by the way) and I burned the potatoes … and you were talking to the fellow who used to be an embalmer … the one who was telling you about the Annual Embalmers Ball …*', while they're yelling, 'Get to the point woman!').

So what we do (unless your name is Debra or Louise!) is edit the deep structure in three ways:

1 We select a small part of what we know and leave out the majority
2 We then simplify what we are going to say, leaving out words or phrases that may not help our listener
3 We generalise

Of course, while this is a useful human communication trait, it presents real dangers in that when we are listening to people we are actually not hearing the full story. So NLP teaches us, first, to ensure that we are not assuming the meaning we assign to the words the individual is using is the same as the meaning they had in mind. Second, it challenges us to test our full understanding of what they are saying by asking them questions which illicit more information. For example:

Speaker: 'I'm sick to death of busy do-gooders trying to tell me how to do my job! They must think I'm an idiot.'

NLP listener: 'Who is telling you? What is it that they are doing that makes you think they are do-gooders? What are they telling you to do differently in your job? What leads you to believe that they think you are an idiot?'

This approach is based on something called the Meta Model which was developed by the founders of NLP, John Grinder and Richard Bandler. The Meta Model is essentially a way of questioning which helps to elicit the deeper meaning and more clarity from the speaker for the listener. The Meta Model says, in brief:

1 Never ask 'why?'. 'Why' is an unhelpful word which leads people to create new stories and give great long explanations rather than eliciting the actual facts of the situation
2 Seek to clarify meaning: use questions to find out exactly what people are really thinking
3 Expand your choices: if you elicit more meaning or give more specific information yourself, you create choices for both you and your listener in how you react

For example, one of the common things that people do when they are communicating is generalise, such as saying, 'People don't like the decisions you are making'. You, the listener, using NLP techniques, would clarify by asking, 'Which people and what decisions specifically are they unhappy about?'

Congruence/discongruence

Congruence in the context of communication means that your body language and tone of voice are in tune with your internal feelings and emotions. Discongruence, therefore, means that they are not.

People are extremely good at picking up on body language. In fact, we do it unconsciously and automatically all the time. We can tell what sort of mood someone is in simply by observing their posture and facial expressions. And we can tell when someone is 'faking' a smile. You have to be extremely practised in order to 'lie' about your real emotional state, because despite our words our bodies have a way of 'leaking' how we feel.

If you are a skilled communicator not only will you notice the emotional state that someone is in, you will also adapt your behaviour to fit in with it. That means that you might lower your voice to talk to someone who is clearly feeling a bit low in order to establish a rapport which might then help you to elicit what is wrong with them. A cheery 'What's with the long face then?' is much less likely to work than a quiet 'You seem a bit down. Is there anything wrong?'.

However, I do think that NLP, while very good in many ways, gets some of the detailed business about building rapport a little wrong. One of the tools NLP talks about is 'matching'. For example, if someone is shouting at you, you reply in the same volume and tone as them. In NLP training many people find this difficult to do and that is because it simply doesn't 'feel' right to match someone's behaviour unless you genuinely feel it too. If you don't, shouting simply makes you feel like a fraud – and that becomes obvious to the other person, which is when they begin to feel patronised. This is an example of discongruence, as our external behaviour does not reflect our internal feelings – and human beings are extremely skilled in picking up on discongruent behaviour.

If you are unable to match someone's tone without being discongruent, then don't. It's not rapport-building if they think you are faking it. Much better simply to ask in a straightforward tone what the matter is – even if they are shouting.

So to be able to influence people, it is important to have a basic understanding of how people see the world in very different ways and how this influences their thinking.

> **REMEMBER:**
> - People have different mental models of the world
> - The type of language you use makes a difference to how well you can influence someone
> - By observing someone's eye movements you can get a fairly good idea of what mental map they are using
> - Don't assign meaning to others' words – they may not interpret the words in the way that you do
> - Be congruent in your communication

5 Motivation matters

I do not try to dance better than anyone else.
I only try to dance better than myself.
Mikhail Baryshnikov, Russian ballet dancer

Outcomes

After reading this chapter you will:
- **Understand basic motivational theory**
- **Know how to motivate yourself**
- **Know how to create the conditions for others to motivate themselves**

When I was being taught managerial skills over 20 years ago I was told that one of the duties of a manager was to motivate people. And I was taught that the manager can control the motivational levels of other people.

Over time I have come to realise that the latter is a bit of an urban myth, or at the very least only partly true. My experience has shown me that managers can definitely actively demotivate people but that positive motivation is much harder to achieve.

I now believe that the primary motivational force comes from within, not without. We can control our own levels of motivation ourselves. Of course there will always be outside influencers, but if we learn what motivates us and how to manage our own motivation levels, we will be considerably happier in the longer term.

There are probably some common motivators for people: they want to feel good about themselves; they want to be liked and respected; they want to be understood; they want to feel a sense of achievement; they want their effort and special qualities to be acknowledged and recognised. Well, that's all well and good but the problem is that even though those motivators are fairly common, the actual things that trigger those good feelings will differ.

Some people feel good about themselves if they're the centre of attention; some feel good about themselves if they just quietly get on with stuff; some want to be popular with everyone; some just want one or two close friends; some set higher standards for themselves than others; and some set higher standards for others than themselves.

Do you honestly know what motivates you?

What is motivation?

Motivation is what makes a person want to do something – the key word being *want*. And this includes doing jobs that they hate or find boring. A simple definition is 'getting people to do those things that need to be done willingly and well'.

It is quite easy to distinguish those people who are motivated from those people who are not. It is also important to distinguish between being demotivated and being unmotivated. Demotivated people may have had the desire to do a particular job but have lost the motivation. Unmotivated people may generally be quite motivated in the work but have no desire to do a particular task.

Characteristics of motivated, demotivated and unmotivated people

Motivated	*Demotivated*	*Unmotivated*
Asks questions for clarification	Asks rhetorical questions which are unanswerable	Doesn't ask questions
Seeks to solve problems	Points problems out to others	Ignores problems
Wants to share knowledge with others	Wants to complain about difficulties to others	Doesn't talk about the task/job at all
Puts in the time to get the job done	Does the bare minimum to get the job done	Wastes time
Is generally quick to respond to requests	Responds to requests reluctantly	Forgets they have been asked
Seeks to help others	Won't help others and doesn't seek help themselves	Doesn't occur to them that they might need or offer help
Generally seems positive	Generally seems negative	Neither positive or negative because they are disengaged from the task
More likely to cope well with things going wrong	More likely to overreact to things going wrong or complain about them	Doesn't care if things go wrong
Positive attitude to problems – I/we can sort this out	Negative attitude to problems – doesn't think they can be solved	Uninterested in the problems
Keeps a sense of proportion and humour	Gets things out of proportion and can't see the humour	Detached

What motivates people?

There are many different theories about what makes people tick. Many theories of personality are linked to motivation, although the emphasis they place on it varies. For the most part I don't believe that any one theory alone can provide the whole answer.

For example, one theory by psychologist Hans Eysenck says that people have three personality dimensions – extraversion–introversion, neuroticism–stability and psychoticism. Essentially this theory says that people's personalities are linked to their biological make-up and there's not much that anyone can do to change them. For example, if you are born introvert or extrovert, that's it. However, I believe that we can adapt our external behaviours despite our internal personality traits. We can learn to shut up if we're an extrovert or learn to speak up if we're an introvert.

Another theory is that people act as scientists in that they form a theory about how the world works and then test out their theory in their interactions. (See Stephen Pinker for more on this.) This acts as a feedback loop which either confirms or refutes our theories. Thus we take each experience, process it and use it to make judgements about future experiences, so our personalities are formed by what happens to us. This theory says that fundamentally people's motivation is based on their need to predict their environment and thereby reduce uncertainty and increase mastery over the world. This is fine, except that it doesn't allow for the fact that most of us would argue that we sense an 'inner' core of personality which is unaffected or unchanged by external events.

Yet another theory is that people have personality traits which cause them to have predictable behaviour. Personality and therefore motivation is formed by present circumstances, motives and conscious experiences. Again, all well and good, but it doesn't feel that simple does it?

Of the many theories of motivation, there are three that I think are particularly useful to consider in the work context. I outline them briefly below with some ideas about what you might do.

Maslow's hierarchy of needs

Abraham Maslow, who was a founder member of the American Association for Humanistic Psychology, published a theory of motivation in 1954 which I believe is still very relevant to today.[1] In Maslow's 'hierarchy of needs', each need is based on a 'deficiency', that is, it has to be satisfied before the next level of need becomes important. He identified a fifth level of need, self-actualisation, which is only fulfilled when the other four needs have been satisfied.

So what does this theory mean for you? Well, if your basic needs aren't satisfied it is going to be very difficult for you to be able to grow in the workplace in the way in which you would like. From a work point of view you need to ensure that you are receiving adequate recompense, that is, enough to live on, and if you aren't satisfied then your priority needs to be to ask for more money and, if your

[1] Abraham Maslow (1999), *The Hierarchy of Needs*, Chartered Management Institute.

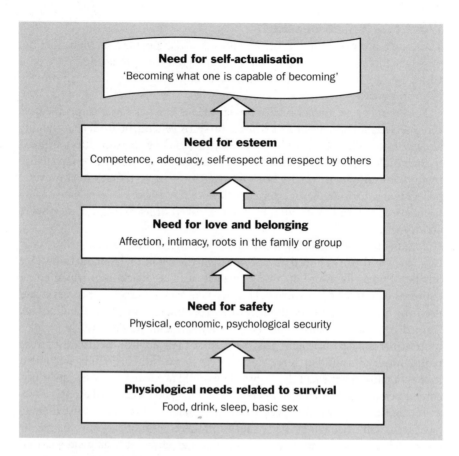

organisation says no, then you need to find a job that gives you enough. I'm not talking here about earning lots of money; I mean enough to buy food, pay your rent or mortgage and socialise occasionally. This is an absolute amount, not a relative one. It's not about being paid less than others necessarily, but about being paid enough to survive.

I worked in an organisation some years ago that announced a series of redundancies. We were told that 15 posts would go from our particular area of work, but that all 30 of us were 'at risk' until it was decided which particular posts would actually go. It was all part of a legal consultation processes and the organisation had to do it to comply with statutory requirements. You would have thought that if people were worried about losing their jobs they would work extra hard to prove that they were indispensable and so avoid the 'chop'. But what actually happened was everyone more or less stopped working because we were spending all our time worrying about our jobs and speculating about what might happen. Motivation and performance plummeted.

In more general terms, it will also help if you ensure that you are getting on well with your colleagues in your team and that you are making the effort to build good, warm, friendly relationships.

And you need to build your self-esteem, which I cover later in the book (see Chapter 10).

Carl Rogers

Psychologist Carl Rogers talked about the conditions for personal growth (the self-actualisation part of Maslow's hierarchy). He said that people are generally dynamic and goal-directed, and that we have two ways of identifying who we are. First, our own experiences of what we can and cannot do and, second, evaluations made of us by other people. He said that most of us need unconditional regard, that is to be liked for ourselves, independent of our actions, which is something often only achieved in family relationships.

We need and want positive regard in the workplace – and for many of us that's not easily achieved, often because our bosses don't realise that's what we need. Also, in reality, can we truly expect unconditional regard at work? Of course not, because what we do has a huge impact on the ability of our organisations to deliver, on how our team functions and on how well objectives are achieved. We cannot and should not expect unconditional regard at work. Yet it's interesting how many of us still expect appreciation even when we know, deep in our hearts, that we have not necessarily done what we should have.

Nonetheless, there are things that we can do to help ourselves here. I list below some of the common complaints that I hear from people at work and some things that you might be able to do to help motivate yourself.

Common complaints

I don't feel valued at work	Ask for feedback from colleagues and your manager – seek praise
I don't feel cared about by my manager	Tell your manager that you feel this way and be specific about what you need
I don't get positive feedback	Ask for it
I don't feel tested	Ask for opportunities to learn new skills

Douglas McGregor's X and Y Theory

Douglas McGregor developed a theory of motivation in terms of Theory X and Theory Y.[2] The two theories represent assumptions that people make about people with whom they work. Theory X assumes that people basically dislike work and need to be directed and controlled in order to produce results. Theory Y assumes that people like work and under the right conditions will seek to take responsibility for it.

[2] Douglas McGregor (1960), *The Human Side of Enterprise*, McGraw Hill Higher Education.

Attitudes to work – the X and Y theory

Theory X	Theory Y
People dislike work and will avoid it if they can	Work is necessary for people's psychological growth
People must be forced or bribed to make the right effort	People want to be interested in their work and under the right conditions they can enjoy it
People would rather be directed than accept responsibility themselves	People will direct themselves towards an accepted target People will seek and accept responsibility under the right conditions The discipline people impose on themselves is more effective and can be more severe than any imposed on them
People are motivated mainly by money People are motivated by anxiety about their security	Under the right conditions people are motivated by their desire to realise their own potential
Most people have little creativity except when getting around management rules	Creativity and ingenuity are widely distributed and grossly under-used

The interesting thing about the X and Y theory is that it can become self-fulfilling. If our manager has high expectations of us it often brings out the best in us. If, however, they don't it can reinforce our own poor behaviour.

So your manager can influence how you see yourself and what you believe about others in work. But here's the thing: if your manager is behaving like Theory X towards you, you need to ask yourself if you, in your behaviour, are exhibiting some of the Theory X behaviours. And if you are and you want your manager to change their approach then don't wait for them to 'motivate' you. Just behave as if you are Theory Y and you might be amazed at how that affects the way you are treated, not just by your manager but by others around you.

You can only motivate yourself

Despite all these motivation theories I do believe that our managers can't motivate us, although they can certainly help to demotivate us. My experience is that only we can motivate ourselves. For example, if you don't like or trust your manager I'm pretty sure that whatever they do won't make a blind bit of difference. And if you hate your job there's not much anyone can do to make you feel better about it.

Motivation, like enthusiasm, is catching. If you hang around with enthusiastic people, you often find that their enthusiasm rubs off on you. It's the same with motivation – don't hang around with the demotivated negative mob. Spend time with people who are motivated and you'll probably find it lifts your own levels of motivation.

So, what can you do to motivate yourself and get what you need from your manager? Here are my top tips.

Environment

Do you have the right resources to do your job? If not, then speak to your manager about what you need. But be realistic: in the voluntary sector resources are often limited and resources are rarely withheld for the sake of it. More usually, there is not the money for them. However, it is always worth asking.

Communication

Do you feel you are being given sufficient information about your organisation and your team? If not, then decide what it is you would like to know and ask your manager if it is possible to create regular team meetings where you can share what's going on.

Feedback

Do you feel you are getting fair and honest feedback about your performance in your job? If no, then, again, speak to your manager. Ask them what they think you do well (and ask for examples) and what they think you do less well. Ask them what it is they feel you could improve on or do better. And listen to what they say. Don't get into arguments if you think they are wrong. Calm discussion is much more effective. And, anyhow, be realistic. If your manager has a negative view of your performance, talking them out of it probably isn't going to work. You need to prove them wrong by your actions.

Opportunities

I hear lots of people complain that they're not given enough opportunities to develop and grow in their organisation. But opportunities don't usually come to you, you have to go to them. So keep your eyes and ears open. Volunteer for things: offer to get involved in projects, solve problems, sort things out. If you show you are willing and enthusiastic you have much more chance of being in the right place at the right time when the opportunity you're waiting for presents itself.

REMEMBER:
- **Don't rely on your manager to motivate you – work on motivating yourself**
- **If you are not getting what you need, then ask for it**
- **Ask for feedback from your manager**
- **Consider how your own behaviour is influencing how motivated you are**
- **If you need something ask for it, ask for it, ask for it ...**

6 Teamwork: it's better together

Whether you're on a sports team, in the office or a member of a family, if you can't trust one another there's going to be trouble.
Joe Paterno, US college football coach (b. 1926)

Outcomes

After reading this chapter you will:
- Understand what makes a good team
- Have a sense of how effective a team member you are
- Have some tools to help you be a more effective team member

---

There are some people who say that they prefer to work alone. Unfortunately, in the workplace, nothing lasting and meaningful can be achieved unless it is done as part of a team. That sounds like a very sweeping statement, doesn't it? But the fact is that even if you sat quietly by yourself and wrote a great policy on volunteer recruitment, you can't implement it without the engagement and co-operation of others. And that is true for just about anything that happens in an organisation. One of the most critical things we all have to learn is how to work well within teams.

However, it's not just loners who sometimes struggle to work well within teams, those people who are gregarious and like to take over can also cause rifts. The point is that it's not always that easy. Sometimes the team leader isn't very good and that makes it hard. Or you don't get on well with other members of the team. Or there are cliques that have formed and you feel left out, and so on.

The distinction between groups and teams

Essentially a group is a loose collection of people with no particular common aim and no agreed ways of operating. A team is a collection of people with specific aims in common and collective ways of working.

A team is therefore two or more people who are interacting with one another in such a manner that each person influences and is influenced by each other person. For a collection of people to be defined as a team the members must:

- Interact with one another
- Be socially attracted to each other
- Share goals or objectives
- Have a shared identity which distinguishes them from other groups

You know that you are working in an effective team if you have the following characteristics:

- A clearly defined goal that everyone understands
- A high level of co-operation between individual members of the team
- A flexible approach to the work so that people do not limit their service to the team to only their personal job description
- Good results!

Team leadership

It is probably true to say that for the most part effective teams have effective team leaders. If you are the team leader then this is what you are responsible for in the team:

- Ensuring that there is a clearly defined goal
- Identifying those issues which inhibit the team from reaching its goals
- Addressing those issues, removing the inhibitors and enabling the goals to be achieved
- Making sure that every individual within the team understands the part they have to play and how well they are doing
- Ensuring that there is plenty of opportunity for discussing progress and problems
- Keeping the team apprised of progress
- Making sure that there is a good communication flow between different parts of the team
- Involving the team in decision making
- Ensuring that there are support mechanisms in place for those members of the team who are struggling
- Dealing with those members of the team who are not pulling their weight or who are in some way disrupting the work of others

If you are not the team leader that does not mean that you can abdicate responsibility for the success of the team. You are, after all, an adult. If you feel that your team leader is not doing the above then you can ask for it to be done. And that doesn't have to be done aggressively or whiningly. Simply saying something like: *'Boss, I've been thinking. It might be quite helpful if we all got together on a weekly basis and had a chat about what we're trying to achieve and what the problems are. It would save you a lot of time and hassle having to chase us up for things. If you think it's a good idea shall I fix up the meeting and come up with an agenda?'*

Phrased well, most team leaders will be grateful for this suggestion, especially if you ensure that you are not couching it in a critical way.

How good a team member are you?

Never lose sight of the fact that the most important yardstick of your success will be how you treat other people, your family, friends and co-workers and even strangers you meet along the way.

Barbara Bush, US first lady

There has been a lot of research and study into what makes teams effective. Some of you will have heard, for example, of Dr Meredith R Belbin, who defined the different roles that people play in teams (see Bibliography). This sort of stuff can, of course, be quite useful in thinking about teams. However, I think that for us, in the context of this book, the most useful thing is to consider how well you do at being part of a team and give you some of the skills that help you to negotiate your way through team working.

Team-membership exercise

This simple questionnaire should help you to identify how well you work in a team environment and some of the areas that would be useful for you to develop.

Visualise the particular team you are working in. Answer the following questions about how you respond within that team. There are no wrong or right answers, and some answers you may need to guess at. You might like to ask a friend or a team member to use this questionnaire to evaluate your effectiveness as a team member. You can then replace the 'I' in the questionnaire with your name before you give it to your friend or team member.

A scoring table is set out below the questions for you to score your effectiveness.

Team-work skills questionnaire

1. I give my opinion on things

a. Very frequently   **b.** Frequently   **c.** Sometimes   **d.** Rarely   **e.** Never

2. I share information freely and without being asked

a. Very frequently   **b.** Frequently   **c.** Sometimes   **d.** Rarely   **e.** Never

3. I identify solutions to problems

a. Very frequently   **b.** Frequently   **c.** Sometimes   **d.** Rarely   **e.** Never

4. I tend to lead the team on what we do

a. Very frequently   **b.** Frequently   **c.** Sometimes   **d.** Rarely   **e.** Never

5. I suggest directions the team can take

a. Very frequently   **b.** Frequently   **c.** Sometimes   **d.** Rarely   **e.** Never

6. I listen

a. Very frequently   **b.** Frequently   **c.** Sometimes   **d.** Rarely   **e.** Never

7. I give positive feedback to other members of the team

a. Very frequently   **b.** Frequently   **c.** Sometimes   **d.** Rarely   **e.** Never

8. I compromise

a. Very frequently   **b.** Frequently   **c.** Sometimes   **d.** Rarely   **e.** Never

9. I help relieve tension

a. Very frequently   **b.** Frequently   **c.** Sometimes   **d.** Rarely   **e.** Never

10.I talk

a. Very frequently   **b.** Frequently   **c.** Sometimes   **d.** Rarely   **e.** Never

11.I give people feedback if I have an issue with them or their work

a. Very frequently   **b.** Frequently   **c.** Sometimes   **d.** Rarely   **e.** Never

12.I participate enthusiastically and willingly in team activities and meetings

a. Very frequently   **b.** Frequently   **c.** Sometimes   **d.** Rarely   **e.** Never

13.I identify potential problems

a. Very frequently   **b.** Frequently   **c.** Sometimes   **d.** Rarely   **e.** Never

Team-work skills questionnaire – scoring

Score by awarding yourself the number of points shown in the table on the following page. Put the score in the score column. Add the numbers in the score column to discover your total score.

Question	a.	b.	c.	d.	e.	Score
1.	3	5	4	2	1	
2.	5	4	3	2	1	
3.	4	5	3	2	1	
4.	2	4	5	3	1	
5.	2	4	5	3	1	
6.	5	4	3	2	1	
7.	5	4	3	2	1	
8.	2	4	5	3	1	
9.	2	4	5	3	1	
10.	2	3	5	4	1	
11.	2	4	5	3	1	
12.	5	4	3	2	1	
13.	2	4	5	3	1	
					Total	**/65**

Results

If you have scored between 55 and 65 your team skills are *very effective.*

If you have scored between 45 and 54 your team skills are *effective.*

If you have scored between 30 and 44 your team skills are *fairly effective* but there is room for improvement.

If you scored under 30 your team skills are *quite poor* and need to be worked on.

Explaining the questions

1. I give my opinion on things

It is important that you have an opinion on issues and ideas in the team. This is because otherwise you leave all the burden of thinking and deciding to other members of the group who are prepared to stick their necks out with an opinion. That isn't fair on them and it isn't good teamwork. Good team workers share their ideas and opinions openly. However, it is also important that you don't take over the team with your opinions, so if you scored 3 for this you need to consider if you are overdoing it and getting in the way of others expressing their views.

2. I share information freely and without being asked

Good team workers ensure that they don't hang on to knowledge but share it openly so that the whole team can benefit from what they know or have experienced. Proactive sharing is the most useful because it takes the burden away from others of having to remember to ask you. If you scored 5 for this, well done!

3. I identify solutions to problems

It is an important aspect of teamwork to be positive and make sure you are seeking and offering solutions to problems. However, again, you need to take care that you are not always the one offering the solutions and therefore not giving other members of the team a chance to suggest their ideas. Also, if they rely on you too much you will always be the one coming up with the suggestions and, to be honest, they won't always be the best ones. If you scored 4 for this, good: it means that you are focusing on solutions not problems. But be careful you are not taking over.

4. I tend to lead the team on what we do

Again this is one to be careful of. If you are always or often doing the leading you are perhaps not operating as a team member but as a pseudo team leader. Effective teams will share leadership on ideas and action. If you scored 2 on this you may need to hang back a bit and give others the opportunity to shine!

5. I suggest directions the team can take

This is very similar to 4. You might not be taking the decision or leading the team but you are willingly offering suggestions. That is good, but again, watch out that you are not forcing the team down a route that they actually don't want to go. If you scored 5 here, then that's probably a good balance.

6. I listen

This is a no-brainer! Of course you must listen. But do you really listen or do you only think you do? What does the rest of your team think about your listening skills?

7. I give positive feedback to other members of the team

This is incredibly important in teamwork. My grandmother used to say that you catch more flies with honey than with vinegar. In other words, giving plenty of positive feedback really does produce tremendous results.

8. I compromise

Actually, this is a really interesting one. In my view the commonly held view that compromise is always the best thing to do is a terrible misconception. If you think you are right you need to stand up for what you believe in. So often people compromise and you end up with something less good than it could have been. Compromise is the enemy of excellence. Of course you need to compromise sometimes but if you scored 5 on this one you need to ask yourself if you are not just wimping out for the sake of a quiet life.

9. I help relieve tension

If you scored 2 or 3 here you are in danger of either being too flippant or taking things too seriously. It is important to laugh and joke within the team. But it is also important to know when flippancy and joking are going to move things along and when they are going to get in the way. However, in the same way that the constant joker can disrupt the dynamics of the team, so can the person who never laughs, always looks serious and moves people back to the point too quickly.

10. I talk

If you scored either 2 or 3 here there is a chance that you are taking up all the airspace. It is important to contribute – but it is so much more important to listen. Which is why a 5 means that you probably have the balance right.

11. I give people feedback if I have an issue with them or their work

You might be surprised that the high score of 5 here is against 'Sometimes' and that 'Very frequently' only scored 2. Again, this is because there is a danger that you are over-focusing on people's mistakes or weaknesses and not making allowances for them being who they are. If you are frequently having to tell people that there is a problem there may well be something about you and your approach that is the problem. Sometimes it is good to give people feedback and sometimes the wise thing to do is to let it go.

12. I participate willingly and enthusiastically in team activities and meetings

Again, a no-brainer. Good team members are positive and enthusiastic and are willing to be open-minded, give things a go and try to make things work. They also understand that it is important to spend time together as a team in order to help build relationships.

13. I identify potential problems

If you scored 2 here you are in danger of giving the impression that you only focus on the problems and not the solutions. Clever team members, even if they have identified the problem, will not necessarily point it out but might ask an open question such as 'Any issues that we are unaware of?' or 'What would happen if …?' and allow other members of the team to identify potential problems, particularly affecting their own work.

How to be a good team member

> *Don't walk in front of me, I may not follow.*
> *Don't walk behind me, I may not lead.*
> *Just walk beside me and be my friend.*
>
> Albert Camus

I suspect most of us would like other members of our teams to say that they enjoy working with us. And I suspect many of us think that they already do. But how true is that really? We will generally think of ourselves as good and useful members of our teams. But you will be amazed what people say about us behind our backs. The problem in teams, of course, is that usually we are all on more or less the same level, and we have to work closely together. That makes it extremely difficult for team members to be able to give honest feedback to each other about how good they are at being a member of a team.

I want to illustrate this point with a real example (although the names have been changed to protect the innocent!). I worked in an organisation many years ago in a small team of six, including our team leader, Tracey. We all worked in a shared office, apart from our team leader who had a small office down the corridor. We generally got on very well but there was one member of the team, whom I shall call Laura, who was a perennial whinger. Now, we all used to have the occasional moan about work – that's quite normal – but Laura was extreme. When things were going well she was fine to work with, but when things went wrong, especially if they affected her particular work, she used to go ballistic. Of course, as we all know, things frequently go wrong, so Laura used to spend the better part of every day complaining or shouting. It was exhausting for us listening to her, so goodness knows what it was like for her!

Anyhow, a very young man called Jason joined our team. Jason was great, he worked hard and was good fun, but because he was inexperienced he tended to make quite a few mistakes. We all understood that he was on a very steep learning curve and made allowances for him. Laura, however, didn't. On one particular occasion Jason had given Laura some information which turned out to be wrong. Laura went beserk. She launched into a tirade of abuse at Jason, called him 'a bl**dy incompetent waste of space' and stormed out of the room, slamming the door behind her. We all witnessed it and Jason was so upset he actually cried. The problem was, of course, that this wasn't a one-off. Laura was constantly storming off or shouting about how dreadful everything was. She really used to drain our team energy, but we generally just ignored it.

However, this time it was different. None of us felt that Jason deserved to be spoken to like that regardless of the mistake he had made. I was elected to speak to Tracey about the incident because the rest of the team felt that this time Laura had gone too far. So I did. She called Jason in to ask him about the incident and he refused point blank to confirm what had happened. He said that he was fine, he was a big boy and he had made a mistake so Laura had a right to be upset.

We were horrified and asked him why he hadn't told the truth. He said there were three reasons. The first was that he felt that by getting so upset about it when the rest of us just put up with her it made him look weak and stupid. The second reason was that if Laura found out that he had told our team leader about the incident she would behave even more badly towards him. And the third reason was that he didn't want the rest of the team to think that he was the kind of person who would complain about another member of the team – he felt it was more important to keep our trust than to tell the truth about Laura.

This is a true story about an individual case, but it can be applied to many organisations. How many of you work alongside a Laura whose poor behaviour and lack of team spirit you just ignore because it is easier than confronting it? The fact is, we the team were as much at fault as Laura. By ignoring her behaviour we condoned it, so she continued to think that it was acceptable because she was never challenged. We made it difficult for other members of the team to deal with her because we didn't tackle her ourselves. And, of course, she never misbehaved in front of our team leader, so Tracey didn't know or even if she did know about it she couldn't deal with Laura because she had no evidence other than hearsay and none of us would tell her the truth.

In the end Tracey moved into our office with us. Laura behaved very well for about a month and then forgot the presence of the boss and had a barney again. She was sacked in the end for unprofessional, bullying behaviour. But if we had dealt with it early enough, maybe Laura would have learned to behave more appropriately and in a more adult-like way, and would thus have avoided losing her job.

All this leads me to ask two questions: first, do you have a Laura that you are not dealing with, and, second, are you Laura?

Being part of a winning team

> *It isn't much good having anything exciting if you can't share it with somebody. It's so much more friendly with two.*
>
> Winnie the Pooh, A. A. Milne

If you want to be seen as a good team member there are a number of things you can do:

- Make an effort to understand what other people's contribution to the team is. You don't necessarily have to know how to do their job; you just need to appreciate how it helps you all achieve your goal.
- If something goes wrong, focus on what can be done to sort it out.
- Avoid blaming other members of the team for things going wrong. It doesn't help solve the problem and it certainly doesn't promote a good team spirit.
- Be helpful to others.
- Be understanding of others' mistakes. You would want them to be understanding about yours.
- Offer to help other members of the team whenever you can. The fact is that if you are helpful, they will want to be helpful back. And if you have a reputation for being unhelpful … well, I'll leave you to work out for yourselves what response you'll get when you need help!
- If a member of the team is behaving inappropriately don't wimp out! Don't leave it to others to deal with. Give that individual feedback in an open and honest way (see some tips on page 68).
- Stop whingeing or at least confine it to the pub! Constantly complaining at work drains the energy and hope out of the rest of the team. No one wants to work alongside someone who is continually moaning. The occasional moan is normal, but the truth is that most of us would prefer to work alongside someone who is cheerful, positive and solution-oriented.
- If you hate the job/the organisation/the boss that much, do yourself and everyone else a favour and leave.

Doing it together

A useful tool I have found for getting a team to think about whether it works well together is using a questionnaire to stimulate discussion and debate. The idea is that each member of the team completes it at, say, the beginning of a team meeting. When all the questionnaires are completed you then all go round and share your scores. (Best to do this one question at a time in my experience.) If all the scores are roughly the same and over 7 then you are probably doing OK. If all the scores are roughly the same and are 6 or below then open it up to discussion by asking people why they put the particular score that they did. If there are some scores that are widely different then, again, ask individuals to explain why they scored that particular question in the way that they did. You then discuss what needs to change in order for the scores to match and to be at the higher end.

The great thing about discussing teamwork this way is that it enables people to give open and honest feedback about how they think the team and individuals within it are doing without making it sound like a big deal because it is part of a general conversation and everyone gets to have their say. If you are the team leader you can introduce this yourself at your next team meeting – but it is important that you don't argue with people's scores! Their perception is just as valid as yours or anyone else's. The point of this exercise is not to convince people that they are wrong, but to open the team up to discussing differing views and what the team can do so that every member feels valued and engaged. If you are not the team leader, you could still suggest this to your boss.

The questions I have included are general ones which may be helpful. However, there is nothing to stop you adapting this questionnaire to suit your own particular circumstances.

Sample team self-assessment questionnaire

1. Members of the team openly tell other members if they have an issue with them.

Low				Medium					High
1	2	3	4	5	6	7	8	9	10

2. Members of the team do not discuss one another behind each other's backs.

Low				Medium					High
1	2	3	4	5	6	7	8	9	10

3. The team works together to solve problems.

Low				Medium					High
1	2	3	4	5	6	7	8	9	10

4. **Team members have a high level of empathy and co-operation with one another.**

Low				Medium					High
1	2	3	4	5	6	7	8	9	10

5. **The team visibly acts as a united team throughout the organisation.**

Low				Medium					High
1	2	3	4	5	6	7	8	9	10

6. **Individual members of the team think about implications on the wider team when making decisions.**

Low				Medium					High
1	2	3	4	5	6	7	8	9	10

7. **Individual members of the team take steps to manage the wider implications of their decisions.**

Low				Medium					High
1	2	3	4	5	6	7	8	9	10

8. We as a team take difficult decisions and stand by them.

Low				Medium					High
1	2	3	4	5	6	7	8	9	10

9. **We as a team are setting a good example to the rest of the organisation.**

Low				Medium					High
1	2	3	4	5	6	7	8	9	10

10. **Once a decision has been made, members of the team support it publicly, even if they don't agree with it.**

Low				Medium					High
1	2	3	4	5	6	7	8	9	10

Giving and receiving feedback within the team

Good teamwork requires individuals in teams to be able to give each other open and honest feedback about their work and about how they are interacting with other members of the team.

Feedback can go wrong for many different reasons:

- You wait until you are really angry before you say anything and then handle it badly
- You don't say anything at all but just simmer resentfully
- You don't 'own' the feedback – in other words you say things like *'People think that you are a little bit aggressive in team meetings'*

- You personalise the feedback so that the individual feels deeply hurt
- You don't allow the individual to give their point of view
- You do it in public
- You wimp out when you see people getting upset
- You use wishy-washy unclear phrases so that the individual is not really sure what the problem is
- You don't think in advance about what it is you want to achieve from your feedback

The fact is that negative feedback hurts and that is one of the reasons why it is so difficult to give and so hard to receive. You will often hear people say that they didn't want to say something because they didn't want to hurt the other person's feelings, when what we are really doing is protecting ourselves because we don't want to have to handle the reaction we might get – either hurt tears or angry recriminations. Good feedback is not about criticising someone or pointing out to them the error of their ways. Good feedback means telling someone how you feel about something in a way that enables them to listen and doesn't make them feel that you have written them off as a human being.

So what's the trick? Well, it's not nearly as hard as you may think.

1. Think about what it is you want to achieve with your feedback – ideally of course it is to have the person understand what you are saying and change their behaviour accordingly
2. Choose an appropriate time and place – preferably somewhere quiet where you will be undisturbed
3. Don't do it while you are angry – take time to calm down
4. Focus on what happened or is happening, not on the individual's general character
5. Give clear, specific examples
6. *Own* it. Talk about how *you* feel, not how other members of the team feel. If you don't have a problem with this particular individual but others do, DO NOT be their representative! You work with adults and they should give their own feedback. More importantly, if it were you, wouldn't you prefer that anyone who had a problem with you told you to your face rather than hid behind someone else?
7. Focus on what change you want to see in the future, not what happened in the past – people can't change their past behaviour, they can only change what they do now and tomorrow
8. Ask them what it is that you can do to support them in changing their behaviour
9. Let them have their say
10. Recognise that bad behaviour does not necessarily mean a bad person

If you are on the receiving end of feedback – especially if it is handled badly – don't allow your emotional reaction to get in the way of hearing what actually may be very useful for you to know.

1. Listen carefully to what the individual is saying
2. Don't lose your temper
3. Ask for specific examples
4. Ask what it is that they would like you to do differently in the future
5. Check that they are speaking for themselves and not for others. If they say that they don't have a problem but are speaking on behalf of others, then ask who those 'others' are so that you can talk to them directly. If they refuse to tell you (which they probably will), then you are perfectly within your rights to say that in that case you don't want to discuss it with them, as you would rather hear direct from the person with the problem. They then have the opportunity to go back to the real 'complainant' and encourage them to speak to you directly. However, the wise person doesn't dismiss this feedback out of hand. You will still need to consider whether you think it is valid.

Working as part of a team can be challenging; much like family life it is by no means always easy! But when a team is working well everyone benefits.

REMEMBER:
- **You can't abdicate responsibility for effective teamwork to your line manager**
- **You need to be aware of how your contribution helps or hinders the team**
- **Challenge the behaviour of other team members if it is disruptive**
- **Focus on solving problems, not apportioning blame**
- **Don't whinge**

7 Conflict: the rough and the smooth

You can't shake hands with a clenched fist.
Indira Gandhi, Indian Prime Minister (1917–1984)

Outcomes

When you have read this chapter you will:
- **Understand the distinction between passive, aggressive, manipulative and assertive behaviour**
- **Know some techniques for resolving conflict**
- **Be able to give effective feedback**

There is simply no way of getting through your working life without being part of conflict at some time. This doesn't necessarily mean aggressive confrontation; it can simply mean not getting on with someone or fundamentally disagreeing about some issue, point or way of working.

Unfortunately, people are often unskilled in conflict situations so something that could have been relatively easily resolved ends up escalating into full-blown rows or breakdowns.

So having the skills to deal with conflict at work is hugely important. And the most effective skill in dealing with conflict is assertiveness.

What is assertiveness?

We are all born with natural assertiveness skills. We are naturally assertive when things are going well in a dialogue or a relationship. We find it easy to say what we want, to listen to what others want and to agree to something that we are all happy with.

Assertive behaviour means:
- Expressing your feelings, needs and opinions honestly and openly and understanding that others may have different feelings, opinions and needs
- Being direct and straightforward, without being taken advantage of or being threatening to or punishing others
- Exercising your personal rights without denying the rights of others and without experiencing undue anxiety and guilt
- Thinking about your behaviour consciously in conflict situations

The last point is usually where assertiveness breaks down. The problem arises in situations where we are feeling vulnerable or intimidated or our emotions have got out of control. This is when we revert to our default behaviours.

Default behaviours

There is a subterranean emotional economy that passes amongst us all.
In every interaction we can make people feel better or worse.
Daniel Goleman, US author of Emotional Intelligence

As children we learned ways of behaving that paid off for us. For example, we may have learned that if we had massive temper tantrums in supermarkets we usually got our own way. Or if we quietly sat in a corner and said nothing we would be left alone. Or if we told lies we could 'get away' with stuff. This behaviour then becomes unconsciously programmed into us. For the most part we all act like grown-ups, but every once in a while something occurs which upsets us at a deeper level and that is when we will find ourselves reverting to our default behaviours.

For most of us the default behaviours I am referring to are passive, aggressive or manipulative responses to conflict or stressful situations.

Examples
Situation: The boss asks for a report to be finished and on her desk by 9am the next day.

Passive person
The one who stays late to finish the report, then goes home and shouts, cries and blames the boss for finishing late and being so tired.

Aggressive person
The one who storms out of the office because they have to work late, stays late anyway and slams the report on the boss's desk at 9am.

Manipulative person
The one who comes and cries and asks you to stay late to help them finish the report, otherwise they will be in trouble and it will be the third time they have not met the deadline.

Assertive person

The one who knows they will not be able to finish the report on time, goes to warn the boss, and asks for more time to finish it or more support to meet the deadline.

Default scale

Identify where you believe you are most likely to be in a conflict situation where you have lost control or the ability to be assertive. Knowing this can help you to rethink how you are handling difficult situations. Personally, I start at aggressive, move into manipulative and end up shutting up and suffering in passive misery. You can mark down where you think you are on the scale below.

Aggressive   **Manipulative**   **Passive**

Below is a table that shows what we mean by these different behaviours. The chart on pages 75–77 shows the different stances, intentions and actions that we associate with these four different types of behaviour.

Characteristic	Aggressive/ manipulative	Passive	Assertive
Thought	I'm better than … I'm right You're the one with the problem	I'm not good enough I'm not deserving I'm the one with the problem	We're both important We're equal We both have a problem
Words	You make me angry Who are you to say …? Who do you think you are?	I can't I'm sorry I'm not very good	I believe we can Let's talk about it What do you think?
Actions	Shouting Looking for someone to blame Slamming doors Sulking	Speaking weakly Trying to avoid blame Silence	Speaking calmly Trying to identify the problem Asking questions to seek clarification
Values	Out to win	Try to avoid blame	Focus on the problem to be solved

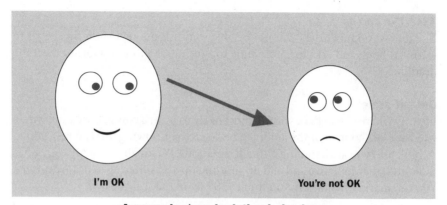

Aggressive/manipulative behaviour

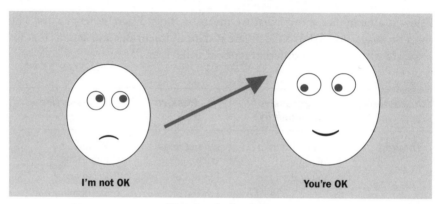

Passive behaviour

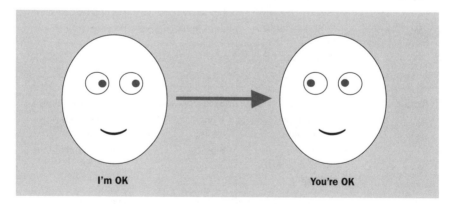

Assertive behaviour

	Passive	*Aggressive*
Basic stance	Failure to stand up for yourself and your rights effectively. Your rights are easily violated.	Standing up for yourself and your rights in such a way that the rights of others are violated.
Intention	To be safe, to appease, to let others take responsibility for you. To rely on the resources of others, get help or sympathy, deny your own needs, interests and resources.	To be 'on top'. Put others down. Self-enhancing at the expense of others. To influence the outcome without being influenced.
Beliefs	I LOSE, YOU WIN, I AM NOT OK, YOU ARE OK. 'I have limited resources.' Victim feeling: 'You will get me if I am not nice.' 'I have no right to ...' 'I cannot contribute much of value.'	I WIN, YOU LOSE, I AM OK, YOU ARE NOT OK. Victim feeling: 'I will get you before you get me.' 'I am right.'
Symptoms/ Behaviours	Whining, apologetic, 'hurt feelings'. Puts self down while placing blame on others ('I am not very good at this, but I might have succeeded if you'd only given me more help'). Overly agreeable, goes along with things. Self-effacing. Downcast eyes, hesitant tone of voice, shifting of weight. Uses 'maybe', 'I guess', 'I wonder if you could ...?' 'Would you mind ...?', filler words 'Uh, well, you know ...', as well as negative responses 'Don't bother, it is not really important'.	Dominating, overpowering, self-enhancing at others' expense, attacking, putting others down. Accusatory, judgemental. Glaring eyes, leaning forward, pointing at people with fingers, using raised tone of voice. Using threatening words: 'You'd better ...', 'If you do not watch out ...'; put-downs: 'Come on, you must be kidding'; evaluative comments: 'should', 'bad'.
Emotions experienced	Keeps emotions hidden, not expressed. Tension turned inward.	Tension turned outward. Expressed with anger, rage, hate or misplaced hostility.
Effect on others	Others feel guilty or angry, trapped and frustrated. They cannot disagree without 'hurting' or being seen as unconcerned or hostile toward the non-assertive individual.	Others feel hurt, defensive, humiliated, fearful, resentful, dependent. They cannot disagree without being seen as either presumptuous, defensive or incompetent.

Short-term pay-offs/ Benefits	You get left alone No one asks you to join in You keep out of trouble	You get your own way People do what you tell them to
Long-term consequences	You get left out You get walked over Your point of view is not sought You end up with all the rubbish jobs You feel resentful	People resent you People are afraid of you You don't get included in things People avoid you

	Manipulative	*Assertive*
Basic stance	Manipulating others so that you get what you want but in such a way that the rights of others are violated.	Standing up for yourself and your rights in such a way that the other person's rights are not violated
Intention	To control and manipulate those around to avoid confrontation and the risk of rejection.	To communicate, influence others, use your resources, to gain self-respect without diminishing others.
Beliefs	Like the aggressive person: I WIN, YOU LOSE, I AM OK, YOU ARE NOT OK. Victim feeling: 'I will get you before you get me', 'I am right'.	I WIN, YOU WIN, I AM OK, YOU ARE OK. We are both responsible. 'I have rights', 'I value my resources'.
Symptoms/ behaviours	Deceiving self and others. Attacks are concealed (unlike the open aggressive person) which makes it difficult for others to pin it down and deal with it.	Expressive, descriptive, firm but not hostile. Using 'I'. Messages are clear. Willing to give information, expressing goals, expectations. Good eye contact, stands firmly yet comfortably, using strong steady tone of voice. Uses 'I think', 'I feel', cooperative words ('Let's see, how can we …'), empathetic statements ('What do you think …?').
Emotions experienced	Denies their feelings, wriggles away leaving others feeling puzzled, thwarted and guilty.	Is aware of own emotions. Deals with feelings as they occur.

Effect on others	Makes others feel guilty if they do not do whatever the person wants.	Feel in touch, informed, enhanced. Can disagree without feeling like attackers, or being judged incompetent. Contributions and influence often increase.
Short-term pay-offs/ benefits	You get your own way People do not argue with you	People trust you You have healthy relationships
Long-term consequences	People do not believe you People begin to resent you You cry too often	People trust you You have healthy relationships

We think and talk of assertiveness when there is a *lack* of it, a special *need* for it. When all goes well, when communication is flowing, assertiveness is natural and is automatic; we listen to others' views; we offer alternatives; we are not judgemental, we agree to disagree; we do not threaten nor feel threatened. *We are in control.*

Rights and responsibilities

Being assertive is about setting a value on yourself and your opinions, needs and feelings, as well as on other people.

Assertiveness means that we believe we have a *right* to feel and express things. And with rights come responsibilities:

1. To have the right to behave assertively is not like having a licence to act in any manner without considering other people
2. Accepting those rights brings personal power, which in turns brings responsibility
3. Our rights to assertive behaviour do not deny the rights of others in any given situation
4. It's OK to make mistakes, but others have the right not to appreciate the fact that you made an error, to feel disappointed and to express their anger or hurt

Assertiveness is about making a conscious choice about how you are going to behave in any given situation. It is about choosing to *respond* rather than *react*.

Children have very straightforward ways of solving problems! They will tend to solve their problem with fight (standing ground defiantly – aggressive) or flight (run away – passive) or by manipulative behaviour such as telling tales or threatening to betray a secret. These are ways of *reacting*, that is without thinking before acting.

Assertiveness means *thinking* about the *outcome* you want to achieve out of a confrontation before engaging in it.

My husband loves to go to the gym on Sunday afternoons and I usually have our Sunday meal prepared for him when he gets home, something I really enjoy doing. There were occasions in the past, however, when he would be home later than he said he would be because he had fallen asleep in the sauna or something, and he didn't take his phone with him for obvious reasons. On the first few occasions this happened, instead of being assertive I launched into the classic mistake that many of us make in how I reacted: yelling and accusing him of not caring about me – you know the sort of thing.

Below I break this down so that you can see what was happening here and what would have been a more effective response.

Situation
Husband/partner comes in late for dinner. You say, 'You are so inconsiderate, you never think about me, you make me miserable and unhappy ...'

Outcome
What usually happens is that you both stop communicating, you both stop listening to each other, and he does not believe you because he does care about you so your assertion is simply not true.

Further, you are blaming him for your feelings, which in fact you own. He is responsible for his behaviour – but not for your feelings about his behaviour.

Consequence
No solution, no resolution.

A more effective response would be:

Explain the facts
'This is the third time in a month that you have got home later than you said you would and you didn't let me know. This means that I've burned the dinner again.'

Own your feelings
'I feel taken for granted and frustrated.'

Focus on the future
'For the future will you please take your mobile phone with you so that you can telephone and let me know if you are going to be late?'

In a working situation, when explaining the facts, you may want to add what the consequences are of the individual's behaviour, as below.

Situation
A work colleague consistently turns up late for work.

Explain the facts

'This is the third time this week that you have been late for work. When you're late I have to answer your phone and therefore cannot do my work.'

Own your feelings

'I feel taken for granted and frustrated that you don't appreciate how much of an extra burden this is on me.'

Focus on the future

'In the future, I'd like you to come in on time. Or can we make other arrangements?'

Assertiveness techniques

Below are some classic assertive techniques that you may find useful in dealing with conflict situations.

Broken record

This technique is useful for when you are clear about what you want to say and you want this to be known. It's a way of helping to gain and maintain control over hostile interactions and avoiding generating more anger. This technique needs a judgement call on your part if you believe the situation could go in circles.

In short, respond as if you were a broken record that repeats itself again and again. Simply repeat one or two short sentences, in the same tone, same volume and same intonation, until the other person starts to hear you. Try to use a calm voice if they are angry. However, what you repeat is important, so choose words that show that you are willing to help, that you are concerned, rather than formal, bureaucratic language.

1. Identify your goal and make a clear and specific statement: *'I won't be able to work late this evening'*
2. Acknowledge the response of the other person whilst maintaining your statement: *'I understand you are under a great deal of stress, but I won't be able to work late this evening'*
3. Repeat the statement without being sidetracked: *'That's not relevant to the main issue, which is that I won't be able to work late this evening'*

For this technique to be successful:

- Be clear about what you will do if you aren't being heard
- If someone listens and acknowledges your point make sure you demonstrate that you have noticed and thank the other person for their cooperation, letting them know how pleased you are
- Since you have decided how you plan to deal with it if they are not listening then there is no need to get upset – keep your self-control, it will make it easier in the long run
- Don't be surprised if you aren't being heard

Fogging

This technique helps to defuse conflict situations especially with aggressive people. It is also sometimes called the 'soft pillow' technique. It is a way to ensure that aggressive behaviour towards you is managed so that the situation doesn't escalate. Essentially, you simply 'absorb the punches' for want of a better terminology. Metaphorically, if you meet a 'brick wall' then both parties get hurt in some way. However, a 'pillow' absorbs the impact and softens everything up.

Basically, just act as if you are absorbing the verbal punches until they have run out. For example, if someone is yelling at you, 'You made a stupid mistake, you don't care about getting things right and you're lazy and incompetent', the fogging technique would be to reply with, 'Yes, I did make a mistake, and I can see why you think that I don't care about getting things right and why you might think I am lazy and incompetent.' Saying these things doesn't mean that you agree with them, but it can help to calm the person down sufficiently so that you can then have a more reasoned discussion about what happened and they are able to put you and the mistake back into perspective.

Example phrases to use in fogging:
1. I can see why you are feeling upset …
2. I understand how you might think that …
3. I can see your point …
4. I'm so sorry you're upset about …
5. It wasn't my intention to upset you …

Giving and receiving feedback

Being able to give and receive feedback is a critical skill in the workplace. It allows you to learn more about yourself and how you are seen by others and it can increase opportunities for others to appreciate their own strengths and weaknesses, to grow and improve on the areas you believe need work. Your feedback says as much about you and your values as it does about the receiver.

Giving feedback – the sandwich solution

When giving feedback it is helpful to do something to create the right sort of listening in the person to whom you are talking. I would suggest you begin with saying something positive – not so as to dampen down your criticism, but to help them realise that you are not saying that they are a terrible person but that there is a particular piece of behaviour that is unhelpful. You then follow that up with the criticism, expressed calmly and focusing on the behaviour not the person, and you end with a positive statement about your belief that they can change this behaviour. For example:

One of the things I really appreciate about you is how passionate you are about our work. However, at the meeting last week your behaviour towards Donna was quite aggressive when she said that she didn't agree with your point of view. For the future, please allow others to have their say without interrupting and understand that all of our opinions are valid even if we disagree with one another. I know that you don't mean to offend or upset people and am confident you can tone it down a bit.

Tips for making feedback effective

- Select the priority areas and talk about them, not all the instances of someone's failings. You don't want completely to demoralise, you want to create a climate that allows them to acknowledge their fault and *want* to change
- Focus on what can be changed (their behaviours)
- Be specific and give real examples of what went wrong
- Be positive when explaining what you want done differently – express your belief that they can change
- Offer alternatives, using words such as 'improve', 'change', 'do differently'
- Own the feedback, using 'I noticed' or 'I feel' – *never* say 'people feel' as that diminishes the power of your feedback and leaves the person with nowhere to go. For example, if you didn't feel angry but you noticed that others did then you can still own it by saying 'I felt uncomfortable because I observed that a number of people in the room appeared to be upset'
- End up with a positive so that the person feels that the problem is not them as a human being but a specific piece of behaviour which they have the power to change

Tips for receiving feedback

- It is vital that you listen. If you can listen first, before discussing, rejecting or arguing, however uncomfortable it may feel to receive it you are more likely to get a better outcome
- Make sure you understand what is being said and avoid interpretations: repeat, paraphrase, etc.
- Check it out with other people rather than relying on only one source of information
- Remember it is your choice to act upon the feedback or not

Setting boundaries: saying 'no'

There are a number of commonly held assumptions about saying 'No': that it is callous, selfish, uncaring, rude and aggressive, abrupt or blunt, or that others will always take offence, feel hurt and rejected. But these really are mostly misconceptions. It's really not the saying 'No' that's the problem, it's the way in which we say it that most often causes the problem.

- Listen to your internal reaction when asked something: if you can answer a definite 'Yes' or 'No', then say so
- If you are unsure about whether you can meet the request , then ask for more time before you make a decision; hesitating can give the impression that you are trying to find a way to say 'No' when that may not be the case at all
- Practise saying 'No' without dwelling on justifying yourself or apologising

- Give a direct explanation, accept responsibility for saying 'No' and do not blame others for you being unable to meet a request
- Remember you are refusing the request, not the person
- Give the other person the opportunity to express their feelings
- Express your own feelings truthfully

Having said all that, you do need to make every effort to meet people's requests. Classic mistakes in how we say 'No' involve people saying things like 'I'm too busy' or 'Why can't you do it yourself?' These types of response just get people's backs up and makes it harder for them to want to help you when you need it.

If you really are too busy then explain what it is you are busy doing: *'I'm so sorry, Satinder, I simply have to get this report written by 5pm this evening because we need to send it to the Board first thing tomorrow morning.'*

Offer alternatives: *'Have you asked Ruby? She said this morning at our meeting that she had some spare time today.'*

Negotiate: *'If you can help me proofread this report, then I will be able to help you at around 4ish.'*

Raising a problem with someone

Before tackling anyone with a problem or issue, if you work through the following checklist before you approach them you are much more likely to get the result you want.

1. Identify what you are trying to achieve

First, are you sure that your facts are right? You will need to allow them to tell you their side of the story. And what outcome do you want to achieve? Do you want to let off steam? Resolve the situation? Let someone know how you feel about something? Punish someone?

It is really important that you are clear about your outcome because it will affect the way in which you handle the situation. You need to remember the long-term consequences of any action you take. For example, if someone has made a mistake and you don't want them to make it again, probably the last thing you should do is yell or make them feel bad because in the future they are more likely to hide mistakes rather than admitting them and dealing with them. Letting off steam may make you feel better in the short term, but could have disastrous consequences in the longer term.

2. Anticipate their likely reaction

Try to imagine, based on your knowledge of them, how they are likely to respond to what you have to say. What seems logical and reasonable to you may not seem the same to them.

3. Decide how you will respond if you don't get the reaction you want

Consider how you will react if they get angry or deny or disagree completely with what you are saying.

4. Think about other ways of achieving your objective

Approaching them directly may lead to a confrontation that neither of you want. Do you need to talk with them informally outside of the working environment? Is this issue really that important to you? Can it be brought up in a team meeting more appropriately? Is there another person who can help you to deal with it?

5. Choose the best time and place

Think about the timing of your conversation. You want to be able to be honest with each other. If the other person is afraid or feeling hassled, or if they are conscious of others being around, then you are unlikely to achieve the outcome you want.

6. Have a 'fall back' position and decide your limits

You will not always get the exact result or outcome you are looking for during the initial conversation. What will you do if this is the case? What are you prepared to accept and what will you do if you simply cannot get your point across or there is no movement from the other person?

Decide your limits in advance. How far are you prepared to compromise? What happens if you find out something during the course of the conversation that you hadn't been aware of or hadn't expected to hear? What are you going to do if you simply cannot resolve the conflict?

Using negotiation skills in conflict situations

Essentially there are two main drivers in how successfully you are able to 'negotiate' the kind of outcome you want: the degree of concern for your own outcome and the degree of concern for the other person's outcome.

With this as the context there are five fundamental styles of managing conflict using negotiation skills. I will share them with you so that you have a range of additional tools at your disposal.

Defeating

This is where we try to convince the other person to accept a position that favours only our own interests. This approach requires persuasion, manipulation, concealment of our true position, and the use of threats and pressure tactics. This may work in the short term but in the long term is likely to damage the relationship and make the ability to work together in the future much more difficult.

Accommodating

With this style we focus on the other person's needs rather than our own. Accommodating may be used to end negotiations, to leave the other person completely satisfied so we can ask for something later, or because the issues are much more important to the other person than to us. This is a good long-term strategy because if you accommodate someone's needs when you are not so set on achieving your own outcome then when you really need something you are more likely to get it.

Compromising

This style is where both people see the conflict as apportioning some part of the 'pie' and therefore settle differences by each ensuring that they get a piece of it. This can be useful, but may mean that in the long term neither person is really satisfied.

Collaborating

This is where both people work together to maximise a joint outcome. The problem is defined in terms of shared goals and interests. Both people work together to invent options that meet both of their needs.

Avoiding

This is where one person neither pushes for his/her own objectives nor shows concern for the other's objectives. The other person will be able to do what he/she wants (if they are not dependent on you for some action), which may cause them satisfaction. However, if they are dependent on you doing something this style is likely to result in frustration. This can be a useful approach if you are trying to avoid potential conflict or where you perceive the issue as unimportant.

Finally, remember that old saying, 'It is difficult for someone to see eye to eye with you if you are looking down on them'.

> **REMEMBER:**
> - **Listen to understand**
> - **Focus on the future**
> - **Choose to respond, not react**
> - **Acknowledge that the other person's point of view is valid for them**
> - **If you've been wrong, admit it**

8 Bosses are human too

What do we live for if not to make life less difficult for each other?
George Eliot (1819–1880)

Outcomes
After reading this chapter you will:
- **Realise how your assumptions affect how your boss treats you**
- **Be able to adapt your behaviour to have a better relationship with your boss**
- **Know how to do well in your appraisal**

One of the classic mistakes that human beings in the workplace make is forgetting that their bosses are human too. I hear time and time again people complaining about their bosses: how they're not devoting their whole time and energy to making us, the employees, happy. After all, isn't that what they're there for?

Well, actually, no. Many of us don't really understand what it is that bosses do and why they sometimes behave in ways that seem to us to be contradictory. The boss is there to achieve the objective of the team or organisation, making the best use of the resources available. Organisations (with one or two exceptions!) don't exist to employ people. They exist to achieve an objective and one of the resources they need is people.

It helps to remember that your boss is not actually a member of your team – they are the leader of it. *Their* team is their fellow managers. They are not your representative at more senior levels; in reality they are higher management's representative to you.

The key difference between a manager and a member of the team is that the manager is accountable for the work of others, i.e. you. They are measured and monitored on how well you do your job, not on how well they do theirs. In fact, the primary focus of *their* job is to ensure that *you* do your work well.

What do different levels of management do?
In a voluntary organisation, with the exception of the very small ones, there are usually around five levels of management, with some expanded levels in very large organisations.

Board of Trustees

Registered charities are required to have a Board of Trustees. With very few exceptions, these are voluntary, unpaid posts. Their primary role is governance: that means ensuring that the organisation is doing what it is supposed to do under its objectivess and complying with relevant legislation. They also need to ensure that the organisation has a strategy to achieve its objectives, and to monitor the performance of the Chief Executive.

They are not supposed to get involved in day-to-day management or activities in the organisation, although the reality for small organisations with few staff is that they often do need to get involved. However, for the most part their role is supposed to be 'hands off'.

Most Boards appoint a Chair. The role of the Chair is to lead the Board and usually to act as the key point of contact with the Chief Executive. It is a common misconception that the Chief Executive reports to the Chair. In most organisations, the Chief Executive reports to the entire Board but the Chair acts as the primary point of reference.

Many Trustees also have other roles in their lives. Many will be in full-time employment or will sit on several Boards.

Chief Executive

There are many different names for this role in the voluntary sector, such as Director, Secretary or Director General, Chief Clerk, etc. but whatever the job title they essentially carry out the same role. They are accountable for making sure that there are strategies, plans, systems and procedures in place that enable the organisation to achieve its objectives. Essentially, they are the 'delegated' officer of the Board and their job is to ensure that the wishes of the Board in relation to the organisation are carried out.

Depending on the size of the organisation they are usually a little remote from the day-to-day activities and rely heavily on their senior managers for information.

They are also usually required to be the chief spokesperson for the organisation and will often have to have a high public profile, either nationally or locally.

Directors/senior managers

The role of the senior management team is to work with the Chief Executive and the Board to achieve the organisation's objectives. They are usually accountable for one or two particular functions within the organisation. They are often dependent upon the information given to them by their direct reports. They will usually feel that they have a certain degree of freedom and autonomy in how to deliver their objectives and will usually be heavily involved in setting the strategic direction for the organisation.

Middle managers/heads of departments

Middle managers can sometimes feel as if they are in a very vulnerable position. They can feel 'caught' between the needs of the senior team and those of the teams nearer to the 'front line' for whom they are responsible.

This is a uniquely stressful position in that middle managers have to deal directly with 'flak' from both sides! They are directly accountable *for* the performance of teams who are 'client facing' and accountable *to* their boss for this performance.

First line manager/team leader/supervisor
This role is accountable for a team with a very specific remit and clear duties. Most of them are day-to-day operational ones. It is through team leaders and supervisors that much of the work of the organisation gets done.

At all levels, from team leader to director, managers are expected to support the management line even if they don't agree with it. There is a very good reason for that. It's because it undermines the entire organisation's leadership if one or two managers talk out of turn. Their job is to put their point of view across in management meetings. If, however, the decision goes against them they are expected to support it.

With the exception of wrong-doing, if their consciences do not allow them publicly to support a position then it is their duty to step down from the management position they are in and, indeed, sometimes to leave the organisation.

This is hard to understand if you are not a manager yourself. However, you do need to respect that they have to be seen to support their colleagues and just because they don't join you in whingeing and complaining about what they don't like doesn't mean that they haven't argued their case strongly at the appropriate time.

Making assumptions about bosses
People can get the relationship with their boss wrong by making assumptions about them that are untested or based on rumour or speculation. Believe it or not, most incompetent people don't get promoted because they brown-nosed their own bosses. They get promoted because it was believed that they were capable of doing the job. Speaking as a Chief Executive, I can assure you I'm not stupid enough to promote someone who isn't any good just because I like them – because I am measured on their performance! And the same is true of others who get promoted to management positions. Just because you don't think they are any good or don't deserve promotion doesn't mean that you are right. Sometimes, of course, bosses do make mistakes when they promote/appoint people, but it's not necessarily because they ignored the competencies and went for someone they liked. It's more likely to be because it's incredibly difficult to make an accurate assessment of someone's ability solely on an interview.

How to get on better with your boss
I mentioned earlier how easy it is to make assumptions about our bosses. And those assumptions can sometimes lead us into behaviours that end up becoming self-fulfilling prophecies.

Of course, in the first instance, if you do have a problem with your boss then you need to tackle it. You need to use your assertive feedback techniques to let them know that there is a problem.

However, you also need to consider whether in fact the problem is being caused by you, your belief about your boss and your subsequent behaviour.

This is where a technique I use called 'the worm cycle' can come in very handy.

The worm cycle

Our behaviour is influenced by our beliefs. If we believe negative things about ourselves or others, our behaviour will reflect those beliefs which will reinforce them. This cycle will continue and we will be trapped in a belief-set and way of behaving that may be unhelpful to us.

For example, if we have a fundamental belief that we are a worm then we are likely to behave as if we are a worm. Because we behave that way it means others are likely to treat us that way. If we are treated that way we feel like a worm, which ends up reinforcing our initial belief.

Most people can't easily deal with this self-defeating cycle at the level of belief. However, you can change your behaviour, which may change how others treat you.

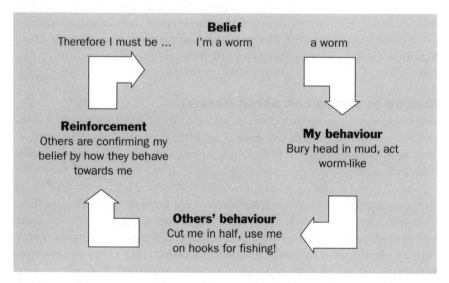

This cycle can be broken at the belief stage, your behaviour or others' behaviour.

It is, however, difficult to get others to treat you differently if you are behaving like a worm. It is also very difficult to change your belief-set simply by deciding to. However, it is relatively easy to change your own behaviour and this is the most effective place to start.

The worm cycle – becoming a lion!

You believe you're a worm but you want to be a lion. The simplest way to achieve this is to change your behaviour to what lions would do.

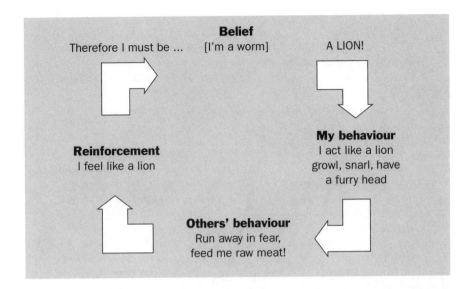

Eventually you may well begin to believe that you are a lion. This change in your behaviour doesn't necessarily result in people changing their behaviour towards you overnight. However, as long as you persist, eventually it may pay off.

If you believe that your boss is an idiot then there is a pretty good chance you are reflecting that in your behaviour, which will in turn cause them to treat you in a certain way.

Again, you need to look first to your own behaviours and eliminate or change those that are reinforcing the situation with your boss that you are in.

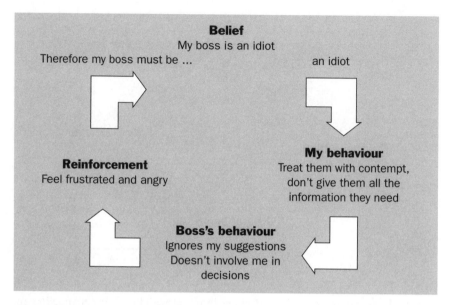

So if you are acting towards your boss as if they are an idiot then they will probably not make any effort to disabuse you of that notion and in fact will take great pains to put you back in your place.

To get a different result you need to try a different tack.

Changing the boss from a worm to a lion

Of course, this is not guaranteed to work. But you have a much better chance of building a good relationship with your boss if, despite the provocation, you behave as if they are pretty good.

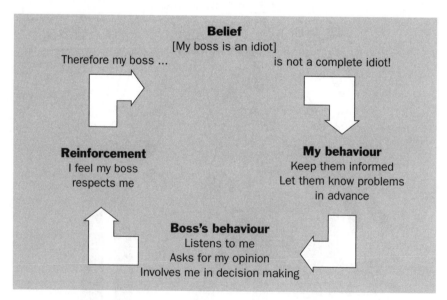

Some tips for dealing with the boss:

- Try to see things from their point of view
- Give positive feedback to them when they do things well for you
- Remember that they value enthusiasm and problem-solvers
- Try to remember that they're not usually evil idiots – they're usually ordinary human beings who have the same worries as you
- Don't think that being nice is being a brown nose
- Don't make untested assumptions about their motivations to become the boss
- Don't make untested assumptions about their motives in their decisions
- Many bosses have not been trained to be good managers, particularly in the voluntary sector where management training is often considered to be a luxury. But that's not their fault so take it into consideration: they are probably learning, just as you are

Managing my performance

It is not your manager's job to manage your performance, even though that's what they will be measured on. If you want to do well at work then you need to recognise that it is in fact *your* job to manage your own performance. And any good organisation will find a way of monitoring and measuring your performance. This section looks at how you can make sure that you have what you need to perform well and also how to prepare for your performance review/ appraisal or supervision (depending on what terminology your organisation uses) so that your achievements are recognised and the areas that you do less well in are identified and plans put in place to help.

Be clear

In order to help you to perform well you need to know the following:

- Who is my boss?
- What is my job?
- What am I measured on?
- How am I doing?
- What do I need to do next?

If you don't know the answers to these questions then you need to find out. You ought, in theory, to have an up-to-date job summary. However, if you don't or if you have kept on asking for one and not been given it, then write your own, answering the questions above, and show it to your line manager for approval. They can then make any adjustments that they see fit. It is really important to have this job summary because not only does it give you a sense of direction, it is also an invaluable document to use in your performance review/appraisal.

A simple job summary might look something like this:

Name of Role: Fundraising Administrator
Name of Role Holder: Kyle Smith
Reports to: Trish Allcock

Key result area	Key tasks	Standards of performance
Administration	Dealing with correspondence	Open post by 9.30am daily Reply to letters within 24 hours
	Filing of documents	File documents according to filing system Filing tray to be emptied at least weekly
Fundraising	Identify potential funding sources	Review new grant schemes monthly Prepare fundraising source report for management meeting

Your formal performance review or appraisal

Why do organisations have performance reviews?
- People need to know how well they are doing
- It creates an opportunity to identify things that are going well and things that are going less well
- The organisation can see what is working/not working
- It's an opportunity to reflect and learn from the past
- It's an opportunity to set targets for the future that reflect the needs of the organisation as well as the individual
- It creates 'forced' time for individuals and managers to reflect on what they are doing and how well they are working together

Preparing for your review
It is sensible to make sure you are prepared for your performance review. This is because if you don't prepare thoroughly you leave the assessment of your performance entirely to your manager and that's not necessarily in your best interests. If you don't already have a system that allows you to complete paperwork in advance then my advice is to write up your view of your performance during the year. But don't be unrealistic or disingenuous about it. It is unlikely that you have done everything superbly so an honest admission of where you did less well is much more likely to go in your favour than wild assertions that without you the organisation would collapse!

I would suggest that it is also in your interests to ask for feedback from your colleagues about how well you are doing. This will demonstrate to your manager and other members of your team that you are aware of the impact you and your work has on others. To facilitate honest feedback, try asking your colleagues the following questions:

- What have I done well during the previous year?
- What have I done less well?
- What should my priorities be for the coming year?

Writing up your own review

Given that you are being assessed on your job performance I think the best starting point is to assess your performance under each of the key areas of your job, using the same question format as above.

Administration

Done well
Correspondence dealt with on time
Standard letter produced in answer to frequent queries
Set up webpage with FAQs

Done less well
Filing not always done weekly although usually up-to-date within the month

Priorities for the future
Ensure filing is done weekly

During your appraisal interview

Although in theory a good performance review should involve you doing most of the talking, the reality is that many managers haven't been given the right kind of training and so they can get it wrong. Most of them won't be trying to be deliberately difficult so you need to make allowances for that.

Hopefully your performance will have been so good during the year that your manager will simply sing your praises for an hour or so. However, in the (unlikely?) event that you haven't been Mr or Ms Perfect Employee here are some tips about how to handle it.

- Listen – don't argue, let your manager have his/her say
- If they say something you don't agree with, first ask for evidence to back up their point and, if appropriate, then reply with evidence that refutes it – CALMLY!
- Acknowledge your own weak performance
- Don't make excuses for things you haven't done well
- Don't blame others – if you aren't entirely at fault then focus on what you need from others to improve on performance for the future, as there is nothing more unattractive than an employee swearing blind that it's everyone else who is at fault
- Be clear about the resources and support you need for improvement in the future
- When addressing areas for improvement look at it as an opportunity to get ideas from your manager about what could be done for the future

- If you are being set targets for the future, ensure that you are absolutely clear on deadlines, standards of expected performance, support and resources
- Ask for any help that you need

After the appraisal interview

It is important that you write up any paperwork quickly. If you don't then you will forget what was said and agreed. It may be that in your system the manager writes up your appraisal. However, it is good practice for the employee being appraised to do their own paperwork and have it signed off by the manager. If you don't have anything that formal then I would still write it up with a copy for you and your manager. This gives you a record of what was agreed.

Questions to ask myself to ensure I have an effective appraisal

- Am I asking open questions which encourage my manager to be clear about my work and performance?
- Am I being patient enough to allow pauses for them to consider their responses to any questions I may have asked?
- Am I really listening to what they are saying, or planning what I will say next?
- Am I listening to them with an open mind?
- Am I open to hearing about their feelings and frustrations without getting upset myself?
- Am I listening to their feedback about how well I am doing with an open mind and without overreacting?
- Am I listening to them with a view to solving problems and moving forward?

DOS AND DON'TS

DO	DON'T
■ Listen	■ Interrupt
■ Ask for and give real examples of work done well	■ Use hypothetical or vague examples when talking about performance
■ Focus on success	■ Brush over poor performance
■ Think about what you could do differently	■ Allow your manager to think that you haven't listened to their request for change
■ Look for solutions to problems	■ Agree with their negative opinions about others within the organisation
■ Be honest in your own feedback to them	■ Focus on the negative
■ Ask for the support you need to do well	■ Argue or justify your position if they criticise your performance

If you are highly motivated then there is a very good chance that you will have a good performance review so the two are very definitely linked.

> **REMEMBER:**
> - Bosses are human beings too
> - Focus on changing your behaviour
> - Be clear about what your job actually is
> - Ask for and listen to their feedback
> - Write up your own performance review

9 Valuing volunteers

It is one of the most beautiful compensations of life that no man can sincerely try to help another without helping himself.
Ralph Waldo Emerson (1803–1882)

Outcomes
After reading this chapter you will:
- Know some of the myriad reasons why volunteers volunteer
- Gather some ideas about how to allow volunteers to feel they are getting what they want out of their volunteering
- Understand how to communicate better with and value your volunteers

Why people volunteer

When indeed shall we learn that we are all related one to the other, that we are all members of one body? Until the spirit of love for our fellow men, regardless of race, colour or creed, shall fill the world, making real in our lives and our deeds the actuality of human brotherhood – until the great mass of the people shall be filled with the sense of responsibility for each other's welfare, social justice can never be attained.
Helen Keller

This chapter is not about the recruitment of volunteers. Learning how to work better alongside them may help in retention, of course, because if you get on well with your volunteers you are more likely to keep them. But given that this book is about working better with people, this chapter concentrates on the volunteers that you have and how you can work more effectively with them. If you do want more information on volunteer strategies then visit Volunteering England (www.volunteering.org.uk) or buy one of the many books (some by DSC) on the subject, or attend a training programme.

I did my first volunteer work when I was 15 years old. To be honest, I didn't do it out of a deep sense of goodness. I did it because my best friend at the time, a girl called Sue Billis, had a deep sense of moral responsibility and she believed we ought to volunteer. It also meant that because I was doing 'good works' I didn't have to go to Mass (at that age even washing people's soiled garments was preferable to Father Janneau's Sunday sermon!). So every Sunday we went along to the local old people's home (as they were referred to then), where we emptied bed pans, changed beds, and read to and chatted with the elderly people there. Sue was much, much better at it than I was. She had more patience and a deeper connection with the residents. I became overly attached to one or two individuals and couldn't cope with the emotion when they later died.

I stopped volunteering because Sue left and there was no one to encourage me to continue volunteering. In those days (late 1970s/early 1980s) volunteer management was not as sophisticated as it is today. The staff and nurses at the home didn't know our names and weren't really interested in us as individuals. They wanted us to do the grotty jobs that they disliked doing (bedpans spring to mind rather horribly!) or tasks like reading to the residents, that they never seemed to have time to do. I never felt valued by the home, I never felt welcomed by the staff and I certainly didn't feel appreciated for what I had done. Having said that, despite the odd cranky resident, most of the elderly people really did value us being there and we formed lovely relationships with some of them. I suspect, therefore, that if the staff had taken our volunteering role more seriously and appreciated it a little better I may well have been motivated to carry on after my friend left.

There are so many different reasons why people volunteer and it's important to remember that, because those individual motivations really do affect how you engage with them. As a worker in a charity very often the cause is all. We may find it difficult to understand why volunteers don't just get on with it and why we have to spend so much of our time making them feel good and important when that seems to distract from what we are there to do.

Not too long ago, I was sitting on the platform during my usual daily commute when a gang of four young girls, aged probably about 17 and on their way to school, came and sat next to me. I couldn't help ear-wigging when I heard them talking about volunteering for the Red Cross. Wow, I thought, this is great! These young people are feeling a deep sense of personal commitment to wider society, actively engaging in thinking about social and economic regeneration: how wonderful they are – and how wrong I was!

The conversation I heard went something like this:

Girl 1: 'So, you volunteering for the Red Cross this year?'

Girl 2: 'Too right! You get free tickets for the Reading Festival if you do.'

Girl 3: 'Yeah, but you have to work long hours for them. I'd rather do a couple of extra shifts at Tesco's at the weekend and earn my own money to pay for the tickets.'

Girl 2: 'Why would you pay for the tickets if you can get them free? That's nuts!'

Girl 4: 'Well, you're not really getting them free are you? You still have to work – you just don't get money, you get tickets.'

Girl 2: [*Long divergence into what her friend's boyfriend got up to at last year's Reading festival … lots of girlie oohs and aahs and 'He never?!'*]

Girl 1: 'I actually really like volunteering at the Red Cross. It doesn't feel like work and I kind of feel like I'm doing something, you know, important.'

Girl 2: 'You are such a suck-up, Natalie! I'm only gonna do it for the tickets. Plus, you get to meet some really gorgeous looking guys.'

Girl 4: 'Are you having a laugh? Like that goppingly ugly one you got off with last year?!'

[*Lots of laughter and teasing.*]

Girl 3: 'Well, I'm not going to volunteer this year. Why would I work for someone for nothing when I can stack shelves for money?!'

Girl 1: [*Quietly*] 'Well, I'm still going to do it.'

Overhearing this made me reflect on how very different people's motivations are and how often the type of motivation affects the level and length of commitment. I would imagine that Natalie is going to volunteer for much of her life. I suspect the others will dip in and out of volunteering depending on what's going on for them at the time.

People volunteer for many different reasons:
- **Robin** gives up most of his holidays to work with Sense, taking disabled young people on holiday because he gets a great deal of personal satisfaction out of it.
- **Mark** volunteers for Crisis at Christmas because his wife died several years ago, he lives alone, has no children and it gives him a sense of belonging, meaning and, most of all, company, on what would otherwise be a sad and lonely day.
- **Linda** volunteers for her local children's hospice because her son died there about 15 years ago and it is her way of thanking the hospice for how well it cared for him in his last days.
- **Gerry** likes running in competitive events and runs marathons because running for charity is a way of getting a place and he figures that raising money for charity at the same time is a bit of a bonus.
- **Carla**, **Sinead**, **Orlagh** and **Jane** are a gang of friends who have a great sense of fun and always do something silly for telethons like Comic Relief and BBC Children in Need because they love the 'craic', they might get on telly and it's all for a good cause.
- **Maria** spent years volunteering for the Samaritans because she really wanted to help people in trouble and she enjoyed the sense of teamwork and togetherness that she got from the shifts.
- **Kerry** volunteers in the local Sue Ryder shop because she can put it on her CV and she quite likes working in the shop.
- **Malcolm** is a trustee of a small children's charity because he used to have a senior role in the City, has now retired and feels a loss of status, so wants to feel needed and important again.

- **Dominic** volunteers for a young person's charity that deals in counselling services because he had a difficult childhood himself and actually finds that he gets personal support and counselling at the same time.

So the reasons are myriad and varied, and not all are purely out of altruism or the goodness of our hearts. Reasons don't matter in the sense that whatever their motivations, these people are giving up their time for our cause. But they do matter in the sense of how we engage with our volunteers. If we want to keep a good volunteer on board we need to make sure that they are getting what they want out of volunteering.

I have identified a number of common motivations from a number of volunteers who I know or have spoken to. I list under them some ideas about what you can do in order to help them feel that their needs are being met.

Career development
- Ask them to identify what aspects of their voluntary work they feel will support their career development
- Encourage them to keep a log of their activities
- Ensure that they get regular meetings (one-to-ones) with their volunteer team leader/supervisor/manager/co-ordinator to discuss what they are learning and gaining from their volunteering, and what the next steps are

Personal need
- Try to gain some kind of understanding about what personal need is being met by asking them what they hope to gain personally from the experience of volunteering
- Make sure there is time for them to talk about what is going on for them
- Include them in social events

Status and responsibility
- Acknowledge their need to feel important by making sure you thank them regularly
- Keep them informed and involved in longer-term planning

Gratitude
- Don't take them for granted
- Keep them informed and involved

A sense of moral responsibility
- Focus on the outcomes and objectives of the organisation
- Allow them to share their values

However, let's face it – some of them we would prefer didn't volunteer for us! Volunteers can be demanding, difficult to deal with, have strong views of their own about what they think is right and wrong, and don't always exhibit the same understanding of the cause or the organisation as we do. Nonetheless, they really do matter. Most of them are wonderful and the truth is that without them most of us would not be able to serve our users or our cause. They need to be valued and cared for.

Valuing and caring for your volunteers

Regardless of their motives, it is important that you make every effort to look after your volunteers, to make them feel involved in the work of your charity, to help them feel that their contribution matters and that they really are making a difference to the work that you do.

There are, of course, different time commitments from different volunteers. Some of them will be regular, turning up two or three times a week to help out. Others may only commit for certain periods and yet others may turn up intermittently. It is too easy both to take the regulars for granted and to ignore the 'casual' volunteer. But, actually, handled well, they will all make a difference to what you do.

Either way, you need to introduce mechanisms for keeping them engaged.

Communicate

Create a mechanism for regular communication with your volunteers – about the work of the charity, its vision and mission, its challenges and successes. You could, for example, produce a monthly newsletter, or set up a page on your website (if you have one) that is only for your volunteers – giving them a special password which only they can use will probably help to make them feel more valued.

You should also try to find ways of communicating with them face to face. Obviously their time is precious and you want them to spend as much of it as possible actually doing the work that they are volunteering for, but pulling them together once in a while for a meeting to congratulate them on their work and celebrate successes will both help to keep them engaged and give you invaluable feedback about your work.

Involve them in planning

When you're thinking about delivering a new service or solving a new problem, ask your volunteers for their ideas. Most of them will have life and work experiences outside that of the charity and ideas that may not have occurred to you. Don't treat them just as an extra pair of hands – remember that a brain comes with those hands, and make use of it.

Solve their problems

For the most part, one of the most important things that you can do for a volunteer is to make it as easy as possible for them to carry out the role that you have assigned to them. That means listening really hard to the issues or problems that they raise and doing everything you can to resolve them. It's unhelpful if there's been a request for a better chair, for example, just to say you haven't got any money. Try to think creatively about how issues which (like resources) can cause real difficulty, can be resolved.

Honour their contribution

It is important to ensure that your volunteers feel their contribution is recognised. They will usually realise that you can't 'reward' them, but organising small treats, even as little as just a bar of chocolate, will help to make them feel valued. Sending them a little thank you card every once in a while or highlighting publicly the value of their contribution makes everyone feel good.

REMEMBER:

- **Volunteers matter**
- **Take time to understand the motivations of your volunteers**
- **Communicate regularly with them**
- **Involve them in planning**
- **Publicly honour their contribution**

---

10 How to be happy at work

If you do not feel yourself growing in your work and your life broadening and deepening, if your task is not a perpetual tonic to you, you have not found your place.
Orisen Swett Marden, US author (1850–1924)

Outcomes

After reading this chapter you will:
- **Know some of the things that you can do to make yourself happy at work**
- **Know how to develop your self-esteem**
- **Know how to exude confidence**

What makes us happy

Happiness is a funny thing. Most of us want to be happy in our lives, but many of us are completely confused about what actually makes us happy. We may dream of winning the lottery; of having a bigger house, an expensive new car every year, designer clothes, first-class travel, luxury holidays; of thinking that having more money will make us happy. And yet empirical studies into the nature of happiness demonstrate a profound truth: what actually makes us happy is not necessarily what we think it is. It takes a great deal of money (which most of us will never get) to produce a marginal increase in happiness, which in any case doesn't last very long, whereas falling in love or meeting a new like-minded friend produces a disproportionately high increase in happiness.

I came across the following interview by John Sutherland on the website *Guardian Unlimited*.[1] He was interviewing Richard Reeves, one of the consultants in the BBC TV programme *Making Slough Happy* and a leading proponent of policies on happiness, not just at an individual level but on a global economic and political scale. He has some interesting things to say about happiness generally.

JS: *You don't go along with the theory that the better-off you are, the happier you are?*

RR: *No. I do, however, go along with John Stuart Mill, who said that happiness is something that comes to you 'by the way in the pursuit of some other worthy*

---

[1] John Sutherland, *The ideas interview: Richard Reeves*, www.guardian.co.uk, 30 May 2006.

> *end'. He also said something that I very much like: that happiness is a thing you must approach from the side, 'like a crab'.*

JS: *So is the underlying message that if you pursue happiness directly, you won't find it?*

RR: *I think that's probably right. But I also think that it comes as the result of what I'd call good purposes in life. The problem with economic striving is that it's really not hedonically efficient. That's not to say that more money won't make you happier. It will. But, above a certain necessary level, it will take an awful lot of money to make you only a little bit happier. It's a very inefficient way of getting more happiness.*

On one level, what Richard Reeves says about pursuing 'good purposes' in life means that happiness at work ought to be really easy for those of us who work in the charitable, voluntary and community sector. After all, we are serving a cause greater than ourselves aren't we? And yet, I come across people in our sector who are not actually that happy in their workplace, despite their commitment to the cause that the organisation serves.

The common things that people cite to me as making them unhappy at work fall broadly into the following:

- They don't enjoy the job
- They don't like their boss
- They don't get on with the rest of the team
- They don't feel recognised or rewarded
- Others are getting promotions and opportunities that they feel they deserve
- They are working too long hours
- They feel stressed and over-stretched

There are certainly external factors that can influence how happy we can be at work. However, I would argue that much of our sense of unhappiness comes from our own cognitive processes: how we view the world and what we want to get out of it.

The other thing about happiness is that, apart from some basic underlying principles such as love, a happy family life, and good social and work relationships, we don't all get pleasure out of the same things. The saying *'One man's meat is another man's poison'* is so apt in the context. My husband, Duncan, is a fitness fanatic. He goes to the gym at least five times a week and absolutely loves it. To me it is hell. I loathe the machines and the atmosphere and the sweaty smells and the grunting. I, on the other hand, will spend hours happily poring over a physics textbook, completely unaware of time passing because I am so absorbed in what I am reading. He would rather eat dirt!

So an important thing to recognise is that what makes you happy is not necessarily what makes others happy.

The actual job itself

The nature of the work itself does not always make us happy. Just because we are working for a charity that is saving lives or the planet doesn't mean that we enjoy the work or that it makes us happy. Charities and voluntary organisations are no different to any other workplace in that what makes us happy or unhappy on a day-to-day basis is more to do with our working environment, the people we work with and our own motivations than the actual work.

The secret to being happy is to know what makes you happy. It sounds self-evident, but it's surprising how many people are not sure about what makes them happy and end up trapped in situations that don't fulfil them.

George Bernard Shaw said, *'Some people blame their circumstances for what they are. I don't believe in circumstances …'*

Happiness at work can be achieved by focusing on what is good about your work or by changing something to help to make you happier. I have also noticed that the higher your level of self-esteem and confidence the more likely you are to maintain a healthy general level of happiness, and also how much more likely you are to keep the bad times in perspective. So developing a healthy sense of self, matched with an increase in confidence, is a sure-fire way to help you feel happier at work – or at least confident enough to find a new job!

Self-esteem and confidence

Marie Curie, the woman who discovered radium, once said, *'Life is not easy for any of us. But what of that? We must have perseverance and above all confidence in ourselves. We must believe that we are gifted for something and this thing, at whatever cost, must be attained.'*

Self-esteem is essentially a term to describe your *internal feelings* about yourself – your self-esteem is not immediately obvious to other people. Confidence is essentially the way in which you portray yourself to others, your *external behaviour* – you may not *feel* particularly confident, or have particularly high self-esteem, but you may come across as being extremely confident.

Your self-esteem is learned during your experiences – and in fact if you are taught as a child to have a low opinion of yourself it can be very hard as an adult to overcome that. You form an opinion about your looks, social ability, physical ability and intelligence from your interaction with people around you. In early childhood you will generally take on board what others say about you as being the truth. Only in early adulthood (from your late teens on) do you begin to question their view and form your own, and even then that only works if you've been given the right kind of feedback – you may continue to have an inappropriate negative view if you have been put down as a very young child.

Much research has been done around self-esteem. The most well recognised and tested is that of Dr Morris Rosenberg of the University of Maryland. He is most renowned for his work on the self-concept, especially the development of self-esteem in children.

Rosenberg says that self-esteem is *'a positive or negative orientation towards oneself: an overall evaluation of one's worth or value'*.

One of his premises is that people are motivated to have high self-esteem and having it indicates positive self-regard, not egotism. Feeling good about yourself and recognising your strengths is not about being big-headed. He says that a person with healthy self-esteem will have positive self-regard whilst recognising that there are areas they are less fond of.

Rosenberg discovered that in the developmental sequence of self-esteem there is a marked difference between the young child and the young adult. Children believe adults' view of them – even if it contradicts what they think about themselves.

In early childhood children are more likely to focus on qualities of character and emotional control. Most of the categories that children base their self-labels on are 'other' dependent. Adults tend to have developed self-labels that are based on their own opinions.

Self-esteem is given to us by:
- Peer group
- Parents
- Other adults
- Teachers
- Experience

Self-esteem is developed primarily through social interaction. Who we hang out with and what they say to us about us is a primary driver of our sense of self.

Nature?

Having said that, I have already discussed in previous chapters the fact that there is an element of 'nature' in our characters. Although there is no proven direct link between our biology and our sense of self-esteem it is probably fair to say that our innate characters may influence our self-esteem because they influence how people behave towards us. For example, if we smile a lot as a baby we are likely to elicit more smiles back. My godson, Ben Layde, was one of the smiliest babies I have ever seen. He is now an extremely confident and happy child who has a lot of friends and still smiles easily.

Nurture?

I've already discussed the point that the environment can either reinforce or minimise our biological predisposition. For example, you may be born with high levels of testosterone. However, if you are raised in a calm, stress-free environment and are taught that taking risks is socially unacceptable, then you are less likely to take risks.

Therefore, if our predisposition causes us to behave in a certain way and people respond to us in a certain way, that will help us to build up our self-picture. If you are pretty or strong or a fast developer or slow to learn or quiet and so on, you will receive feedback from your environment (parents/teachers/peers, etc.) that either confirms or refutes this. This feedback will then go towards the building of your self-concept.

Rosenberg self-esteem scale

Rosenberg developed a self-esteem scale[2] to help people identify how high their levels of self-esteem are. It can be quite useful simply to give you a sense of the areas that you might be able to work on.

Have a go at completing the following questionnaire. Tick the appropriate box for each statement depending on whether you strongly agree, agree, disagree or strongly disagree with it.

	Strongly agree	Agree	Disagree	Strongly disagree
1 I feel that I am a person of worth, at least on an equal plane with others				
2 I feel that I have a number of good qualities				
3 All in all I am inclined to feel that I am a failure				
4 I am able to do things as well as most people				
5 I feel I do not have much to be proud of				
6 I take a positive attitude toward myself				
7 On the whole, I am satisfied with myself				
8 I wish I could have more respect for myself				
9 I certainly feel useless at times				
10 At times I think I am no good at all				

[2] Morris Rosenberg (1986), *Conceiving the Self*, Krieger Pub Co.

Scoring

	Strongly agree	Agree	Disagree	Strongly disagree	Your score
1 I feel that I am a person of worth, at least on an equal plane with others	4	3	2	1	
2 I feel that I have a number of good qualities	4	3	2	1	
3 All in all I am inclined to feel that I am a failure	1	2	3	4	
4 I am able to do things as well as most people	4	3	2	1	
5 I feel I do not have much to be proud of	1	2	3	4	
6 I take a positive attitude toward myself	4	3	2	1	
7 On the whole, I am satisfied with myself	4	3	2	1	
8 I wish I could have more respect for myself	1	2	3	4	
9 I certainly feel useless at times	1	2	3	4	
10 At times I think I am no good at all	1	2	3	4	

Notes on scoring[3]

Scores range from 10 to 40, with 10 indicating extremely low self-esteem and 40 indicating very high self-esteem. Mark your result on the scale below:

10_____20_____30_____40

If you have completed this, the next stage is to consider your result. Does it reflect what you think?

It's helpful to know what your own level of self-esteem is so that you can begin to work on it. The self-esteem scale can help to focus you on what areas you may need to concentrate on. Because, contrary to popular opinion, I truly believe that self-esteem can be built up and developed. Unfortunately, many of

---

[3] The norms for this scale are dependent upon comparisons with a similar sample to this group which can only be obtained by searching the academic literature. The scale has high reliability. Test–retest scores correlations are typically in the range of .82 to .88. Self-esteem is generally a stable characteristic of adults.

us have built-in self-destruct buttons which are quick to react to small setbacks. We have an inner dialogue, which I sometimes call 'The Little Critic'. The Little Critic keeps reminding us of all the things that we're not good at, all our weaknesses and faults, our failings and mistakes in the past.

The Little Critic perpetuates our self-defeating thought patterns. For example:

■ All or nothing thinking – in other words if it's not perfect then it's not good enough
■ Awfulising – this is about turning mountains into molehills, making a mistake, for example, and imagining the worst possible consequences of that mistake
■ Seeing only dark clouds – noticing what's wrong rather than what's right
■ Uncritically accepting our emotions about something as the truth, e.g. I feel ugly so I must be ugly
■ Overemphasis on 'could, should, ought' – focusing on what we ought to be able to do, etc. rather than what we can

So we have to silence The Little Critic.

Silencing The Little Critic

Action 1
Write down on a piece of paper everything about yourself that you don't like. All your faults: physical, social, emotional, professional – anything at all that you are not happy with.

Once you have done that, tear up the piece of paper – or, better still, burn it!

Action 2
I call this action 'Page Threeing'. What I mean by this is that when we see photographs of people in glossy magazines, models and such like, what we see is a model who is perfectly made up, in well-fitting clothes (or not, in the Page Three case!), posed in the most flattering light. When we ourselves look in the mirror (and I have it on good authority that this doesn't just apply to women!) we have a tendency to see only our faults. We peer closely into the mirror and shine bright lights on our wrinkles. We relax our stomach muscles so that our tummies look bigger than they really are and, what's worse, is that we *believe* that picture.

What we need to do is 'Page Three' ourselves, both physically and mentally. And that means not looking at ourselves naked in the mirror unless it's a flattering mirror and the lighting is good (*not* neon!), and standing tall, holding our tummies in at a sufficient distance so that we can't see our wrinkles! Who is to say that that is less true a portrait of us than an unflattering light and 'fat' mirror? Truthfully, most people don't see our individual flaws but the whole picture – our physicality and our character as one part of a bigger whole. Isn't it ridiculous that we will tend to believe the image of ourselves that makes us look bad and don't believe the one that makes us look good? Or that we say that the photographer made us look good if our photo is nice, but that we're essentially not photogenic if it's not a great photo? Aren't we funny?

The same is true for our mental images of ourselves. We will concentrate on what we're not good at, what we can't do, what others do better than us, and so on.

In terms of action, this is what you can do. On a piece of paper write down ten good things about yourself under each of the following categories:

- Physical appearance
- Social attributes
- Professional skills
- Personal skills

For example:

Physical attributes
Good, even teeth
Shiny hair
Neat ankles

Social skills
Friendly welcoming person

Professional skills
Good report writer
Good telephone manner

Personal skills
Good cook
Good singer

And remember that these things are true about you.

Other things you can do to develop your self-esteem

- Spend time with people who think you are great
- Seek positive feedback
- Celebrate things you do well

- Put those things you don't succeed at into perspective
- Give and receive praise
- Accept yourself
- Use the language of self-esteem (i.e. focus on what you did, not how you feel)
- Recognise that no one in the world feels good about themselves all the time
- Recognise that self-esteem can be linked to mood, hormones, environment, etc.
- Stay well away from people who don't help to make you feel good about yourself

Building and maintaining self-esteem

Take risks
- try something that you would normally be nervous doing

Stand up for yourself
- practise assertiveness skills (see chapter 7)
- tell people what you want and don't want

Set personal goals
- set yourself a goal that will challenge you but make you feel good when you achieve it (e.g. join a club, learn a sport, study, make jam)

Learn from, but let go of, mistakes, and avoid perfectionism
- everyone makes mistakes – treat them as learning opportunities
- the failure is not in the falling down but in the staying down

Rely on yourself
- don't rely on others to make you feel good – sometimes they will, sometimes they won't
- give yourself praise and recognition – little 'rewards' for successes

Associate with people who are affirming
- don't hang out with people who make you feel bad or inadequate

Live in the moment
- don't worry about the past – there's nothing you can do about it
- don't worry about the future – it hasn't happened yet
- concentrate on the now – which you can affect

Take care of yourself
- look after yourself physically – get plenty of sleep and exercise
- treat yourself to things you enjoy

Do things for others
- it's very easy to get wrapped up in yourself – by doing things for others you feel good about yourself

Most of us struggle with self-esteem at some point in our lives so those people whom we are finding most challenging at work may also be suffering. And knowing and appreciating that fact can help us to deal differently with those individuals.

You can tell if someone is likely to be suffering from low self-esteem if you observe several of the following signs:

- Scepticism
- Defensiveness – taking things personally
- Unrealistic expectations of self and others
- Unforgiving of self and others
- Focus on limitations not abilities
- Self-shame – keeping secrets about self
- Negative self-talk
- Pride (being too proud to apologise, admit mistakes, admit fear, etc.)
- Inappropriate humility – considering oneself inferior
- Inability to accept compliments
- Idolising others
- Demonising others

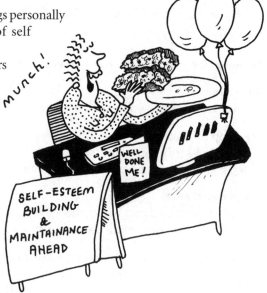

Confidence

Confidence is very different to self-esteem. You can have very low self-esteem and yet still come across as confident. Confidence is, as I said earlier, simply about external behaviours. If you think about the word confidence, the *Oxford English Dictionary* says that its origin is an abbreviation of confidence as in 'confidence trick'. In other words, in some ways you could describe confidence as conning people.

We tend to describe people as confident or attribute confidence to them based on the behaviour we observe and we will assume that because they walk quickly, speak loudly, shake hands, smile and introduce themselves to strangers that they feel confident inside. Speaking personally, I know I give the impression of being extremely confident, but in fact I find situations with strangers quite scary and stressful. I'm as worried as the next person about how I come across! The only difference is that I grit my teeth and act as confidently as I can in those circumstances.

Traits of confident- and unconfident-looking people

Confident-looking people	*Unconfident-looking people*
Walk upright	Slouch
Stride quickly	Shuffle
Speak clearly	Mumble
Shake hands	Avoid physical contact
Sit at the front	Slink to the back
Maintain eye contact	Look away
Smile frequently	Look nervous
Have open body language	Have defensive body language
Introduce themselves	Wait to be introduced
Laugh at their mistakes	Are embarrassed by mistakes

All of us will at some point feel unconfident for all sorts of different reasons.

In dealing with feelings of lack of confidence there are a number of things that you can do:

- Copy the behaviours that you observe confident people engage in (as per the list above)
- Recognise that how you feel and how you appear are not the same thing
- Ignore your self-defeating thought patterns
- Don't accept how you feel as the truth about who/what you are
- Focus on what is good
- Do things that help you feel confident, for example:
    - Wear your nicest clothes now – don't save them
    - Use your good china
    - Make an effort with your general appearance – hair/shoes, etc.
    - Buy yourself a little present
    - Seek praise – fish for compliments

How does this help me to be happy at work?

If you feel good about yourself and are confident in your abilities then you are more likely to take a positive approach to the parts of your job that you don't like. Alternatively, you will consider looking for a different job, or at least talking to your boss about those parts of your job that you are unhappy about. And it's a fact of life: if you feel good about yourself, it's then easier to feel good about most other things!

Optimism and pessimism

Supposing a tree fell down when you were underneath it? Supposing it didn't?

Winnie the Pooh, A.A. Milne

I can't close a chapter on how to be happy at work without considering the issue of optimism and pessimism. Surprisingly there are still a large number of people who consider pessimism to be a helpful trait. They say things like *'Pessimists are just realists and optimists are blind to the reality of life'* and *'Well, I'm just an old cynic'.*

To those people I say 'Bunkum!'. Optimism is not blind – in fact quite the opposite. Optimism is simply about not assuming that the world is terrible and so are the people in it and that all things will go wrong. Who are the happiest people? Optimists. If you are given a new and challenging project to do what sort of person would you rather have leading you or working alongside you? A downbeat, negative pessimist who assumes it will all go wrong or an upbeat, positive optimist who assumes that even if it does go wrong you'll be able to fix it?

Optimists see a half-full glass and imagine it full. Pessimists see a half-empty glass and imagine it empty. Optimists are therefore better people to work with because they will always think that something can be sorted/solved/invented/ created. So, work on your optimism. It will make you happier. It will make the people around you happier – and you'll probably be better at your job!

Moaning makes you unhappy

It's not unhappiness that makes you moan. It's moaning that makes you unhappy.

This is a lesson that really struck home with me during my NLP training. It's a paraphrase of a remark made by Richard Bandler, one of the founders of NLP and one of the trainers on my programme. He discovered, while he was a therapist, that getting people to talk about bad things that had happened to them in the past brought to the forefront the same emotional state that the original thing had created in them. And that re-creating that emotion actually reinforced it for people.

In fact, there is a strong biological basis to this statement. Studies of neural pathways in the brain have shown that the more a pathway is used the stronger it becomes. Talking about things that make us miserable strengthens the connections between those neurons that affect our emotional state – and makes us more miserable! Practice makes perfect in this case.

Further evidence for the counter-intuitive fact that expressing our feelings can actually cause more harm than good is backed up by studies on people who have experienced severe trauma.[4] These studies have highlighted the fact those people who are encouraged to talk about their feelings and experience soon after the event actually take longer to recover than those who simply get on with it. There is something to be said here for the stereotypical British 'stiff upper lip'.

There is of course a difference between 'venting' – i.e. having a quick verbal blast about something that has annoyed you and thus getting it 'off your chest' – and moaning. Moaning is insidious. It damages you by making you more

---

[4] Dylan Evans, *Emotion – The Science of Sentiment*, Oxford University Press, 2001 pp. 82–86.

miserable, as it attracts other moaners which just reinforces your misery, and it drags others down. It seems to be 'fashionable' to be a cynical moaner at work. We look askance at those of our colleagues who, in the pub, talk about how much they enjoy their work and their organisation and what they like about it. We think there must be something wrong with them if they don't go on about what's not right. But it's not that those people aren't aware that their working life is not perfect, it's just that they choose to focus on the good stuff – which is so much better for their emotional health and well-being. I doubt that their life is easier than yours. It's all a matter of how you look at it.

But I'm still not happy at work!

In the end, if you really are that unhappy in your work then you need to change jobs. It's really that simple. And don't be afraid: if you're any good at what you do, you *will* find another job.

Having said that, however, I want to tell you the story my grandmother, Noreen Rimmer, used to tell me when I was a child. It's the story of the Puritan who lived in a town where he was really unhappy. He didn't get on well with the other townsfolk. He found them lazy and irreverent and disrespectful towards him. So he decided to move to a new town. For a while, things in the new town were going quite well. He was welcomed warmly. But then suddenly things began to change. He found the townsfolk here were in fact quite lazy and irreverent and disrespectful towards him. He suddenly realised that the problem was the county. If he only moved to another town in the same county the people would be the same in all the towns! So he decided to relocate many hundreds of miles away to a completely different town in a different county. And again, in the beginning it was great. But then things began to change. He realised that the townsfolk were lazy and they became irreverent and disrespectful towards him …

The moral of this story is that you take yourself with you wherever you go. If you are unhappy, first look inside yourself and ask yourself, is it in fact you who are contributing to your own unhappiness?

And, finally, the Dalai Lama said: *'If you want others to be happy, practise compassion. If you want to be happy, practise compassion.'*

> **REMEMBER:**
> - **Take responsibility for your own happiness**
> - **Develop your self-esteem**
> - **Silence 'The Little Critic'**
> - **Practise acting confident**
> - **Focus on being optimistic**

11 Top tips

This chapter shares some tips from people who generally have good working relationships. Their words are pretty much verbatim and I hope that you find them useful.

In no particular order:

Paula-May Houghton Clarke, Facilities Manager
- Always ask more questions than you answer.
- Always greet your colleagues in the corridor whether you know them well or not.
- Always know the successes of your colleagues, whether they're related to your own or not, and congratulate them.
- Remember that however bad your day is, there's always someone having a worse one.
- Remember that just because it doesn't matter to you doesn't mean that it doesn't matter to someone else.

John Wallace, IT Manager
- Take the p*** (a little). People know when they have been stupid and are usually more embarrassed if you pretend that you didn't notice when they've cocked up.
- Have a relationship outside of work (quizzes, leaving drinks, etc.) – even if you are happy with your circle of school/university/social club friends, make an effort to go out with your colleagues. It will give you more to talk about if nothing else.
- When colleagues are stressed at work, offer to help. They might return the favour!
- Ask colleagues how their weekend was, and listen to what they say.
- Appreciate each other – let people know when you're grateful for their help.

Sash Newman, independent
- Be aware of what your colleagues do.
- Don't just stay at your desk – take time to talk to people.
- Communicate formally and informally.
- Use the nerve centre – the kitchen – for internal communication, notice board, vacancies and fun stuff.

- Read the communications, the newsletters, notice boards, intranet – to keep informed about what's going on.
- If you're not sure about what's going on, don't speculate – ask your manager.

Margaret Lloyd, Chair of Trustees
- Be honest.
- Listen.
- Be open to the possibility that your way isn't always the only (or best) one.
- Ask the stupid question.
- Do what you say you will.

Edwin Beckett, Chair of Trustees
- Make work fun.
- Value integrity, intelligence and frankness.
- Develop your own leadership potential.
- Develop excellent communication skills.
- Admit and recognise that mistakes are an essential part of risk.

Pamela Dow, PR Executive
- If you want to be developed ask for a development plan – it doesn't just happen organically and it reaps huge rewards.
- Patience! Be aware of different individual approaches to activity and different styles, and recognise that there are many ways to achieve the outcome you're looking for that are equally valid.
- Recognise others' individual strengths and that teams are strongest when everyone plays to their different strengths and skills.
- Be consistent in your approach to people of all levels within the organisation – a change of attitude when managing up as opposed to down is always obvious and can often affect the respect your colleagues have for you.
- Act decisively – often a wrong decision is better than no decision at all, and the damaging effect on a team of inaction is often underestimated.

Bridget Gardiner, Director of Fundraising and Marketing
- Try to achieve consensus with your peers, and stick together during rough times and periods of change.
- Say thank you to volunteers every time they help your organisation.
- Spread a little good news every week.
- Be even-handed when giving out praise – success is rarely down to just one individual.
- Let volunteers know what difference their help is making. Update them on service delivery.

Sarah Westlake, Marketing and Production Assistant
- Be nice; treat others as you would be treated.
- Make suggestions to improve things.

- Respect the opinions of others.
- Take people out for lunch on their first day.
- Before you speak an angry word count to ten.

Beth Murphy, Librarian
- Always say good morning before getting into work business.
- Don't blame others and hold grudges.
- Don't bitch about colleagues (but managers are fair game!).
- See yourself as part of a team.
- Make plentiful cups of tea.

John Hoare, Financial Consultant
- Be sure who benefits from your action.
- Remember that customers/clients come first and second and probably third as well (concurrently)!
- Deliver what you promise.
- Prioritise what you do.

Paul Farmer, Chief Executive, MIND
- People are your most valuable asset – prioritise recruitment. It's your best chance to get it right.
- If you need to discuss an issue, do it face to face or on the phone, not by email.
- Be the change you wish to achieve – if you want to raise standards, start with your own behaviour.
- Be clear about passing on work – don't dump the things you don't want to do.
- Keep grounded – spend time with your beneficiaries on a regular basis.
- Identify five key external contacts and invest in building close relationships with them.

Sue Crockford, independent film-maker
- Keep a sense of humour and perspective.
- Be energetic and enthusiastic – people remember those qualities.
- Don't be afraid of demonstrating commitment to your project.
- Don't worry if you don't get every fact right.
- Laugh at yourself – at least daily!

And finally my own top tips!
- Seek first to understand before being understood.
- Start by looking at your own behaviour – is what you do helping or hindering your relationships at work?
- Don't communicate by electronic means unless you absolutely have to – take the time to go and talk to people; that's how you build up relationships.
- Don't bitch about people behind their backs – they always find out and it doesn't help you to create a good relationship.
- If you have a problem with someone, talk to them about it. You'd want them to do the same for you.

Bibliography

Adams, Scott, *The Dilbert Principle*, Boxtree, 2000

Allcock, Debra, *High Flying*, The Industrial Society, 1990

Allcock, Debra, *Do Yourself a Favour: How to be Successful at Work*, The Industrial Society, 1992

Belbin, R. Meredith, *Team Roles at Work*, Butterworth-Heinemann Ltd, 2003

Berne, Eric, *Games People Play: The Basic Handbook of Transactional Analysis* Ballantine Books, 1996

Butcher, Mark, *Achieve*, Directory of Social Change, 2003

Capra Fritjof, *The Web of Life: A New Scientific Understanding of Living Systems*, Anchor, 1997

Carnegie, Dale, *How to Win Friends & Influence People*, Pocket, 1998

Dyer, Fraser and Jost, Ursula, *Recruiting Volunteers*, Directory of Social Change, 2002

Evans, Dylan, *Emotion: The Science of Sentiment*, Oxford University Press, 2001

Exley, Helen, *Wisdom of the Millennium*, Exley Publications, 1999

Goleman, Daniel, *Emotional Intelligence*, Bantam, 2005

Goleman, Daniel, *Social Intelligence*, Hutchinson, 2006

Greenfield, Susan, *The Private Life of the Brain*, Allen Lane/Penguin Press, 2000

Harris, Thomas A., *I'm OK, You're OK*, Arrow, 1995, Avon, 1976

Johnson, Dr Spencer, *Who Moved My Cheese?*, Vermillion, 1999

LeDoux Joseph, *The Emotional Brain: The Mysterious Underpinnings of Emotional Life*, Phoenix Press, 2004

Maslow Abraham, *The Hierarchy of Needs*, Chartered Management Institute, 1999

McGregor, Douglas, *The Human Side of Enterprise*, McGraw Hill Higher Education, 1960

Mill, John Stuart, *On Liberty and Other Essays*, Oxford University Press, 1991

Milne, A. A. and Shepard, E. H., *Winnie-the-Pooh's Little Book of Wisdom*, Methuen, 1999

Moores, Roger, *Managing for High Performance*, The Industrial Society, 1994

O'Connor, Joseph and Seymour, John, *Introducing NLP*, HarperCollins, 2003

Pinker, Stephen, *How the Mind Works*, Penguin, 1997

Robinson, David (ed.), *Neurobiology (Biology: Brain & Behaviour, 2)*, Springer-Verlag/Open University Press, 1998

Rosenberg, Morris, *Conceiving the Self*, Krieger Pub Co, 1986

Stevens, Richard, *Understanding the Self*, Sage Publications, 1996

Whatson, Terry and Stirling, Vicky (eds), *Development and Flexibility (Biology: Brain & Behaviour, 2)*, Springer-Verlag/Open University Press, 1998

Zeldin, Theodore, *Conversation: How Talk Can Change Your Life*, Harvill Press, 1998

Index